AUDREY
HEPBURN

AUDREY HEPBURN

CAROLINE LATHAM

PROTEUS PUBLISHING LONDON & NEW YORK

PROTEUS BOOKS is an imprint of
The Proteus Publishing Group

United States
PROTEUS PUBLISHING CO.INC.
9 West 57th Street, Suite 4503
New York, NY 10019

distributed by:
CHERRY LANE BOOKS CO. INC.
PO Box No. 430,
Port Chester, NY 10573

United Kingdom
PROTEUS BOOKS LIMITED
Bremar House
Sale Place
London W2 1PT

ISBN 0 86276 154 9 (paperback)
ISBN 0 86276 155 7 (hardback)

First published in US 1984
First published in UK 1984

Photocredits: Kobal, Flashbacks, Camera Press, Joel Finler Collection, Aquarius, Rex Features.

Editor: Nicky Hodge
Designed by: Damian Wayling
Art Direction by: Rocking Russian
Typeset by: SX Composing, Rayleigh, Essex
Printed in Great Britain
by Blantyre Printing & Binding Co., Glasgow

CONTENTS

INTRODUCTION

Audrey Hepburn's first starring role was in *Roman Holiday*, which was released in the summer of 1953. During the course of the next fourteen years, she made seventeen more films. Out of these eighteen films in which she starred, seven were among the top money-making films in the year of their release. Her performances netted her a total of five Oscar nominations. She has won one Oscar and one Tony award; she has won the British Academy Award twice; she has won two New York Film Critics' awards and one Golden Globe award; she has been on the international list of Best-Dressed Women five times; during the Fifties and Sixties, she was frequently cited on lists of "Most Admired Women" whenever any opinion-taker cared to inquire.

These statistics are certainly impressive, but they still don't convey the extent of the impact Audrey Hepburn has made on our eyes and minds. She is a fine actress, but she is also much more. She *represents* something – a look, an attitude, most of all a modern way of thinking about femininity.

Broadly speaking, Hepburn fits into the category of the gamine, a type that emerged after World War II – some observers believe the look was a sort of sentimentalization of certain aspects of war-time deprivation; others suggest it was a reaction against the strong autonomous image of the female war worker epitomized by Rosie the Riveter. Whatever the reasons for its psychological and social appeal, the gamine type began to spring up in the late Forties and early Fifties. Edith Piaf was a forerunner of the type. Leslie Caron was a balletic version with a high-energy appeal; Julie Harris was a quiet, more withdrawn version. Shirley MacLaine was a pouty sexy gamine; in some of her early movies, Sophia Loren contrived to put the head of a gamine on the body of a seductress. As can be seen from this mention of other examples, the type was generally European in flavour. It was the opposite pole from the blonde sex goddess, and the gamine image was often tinged with intellectual overtones, or dedication to some principle or goal.

Working within this broad archetype, Audrey Hepburn created something that was completely individual – a new type of which she is to date the only actual example. Just as scientists sometimes find they must create a whole new species just to contain a single individual specimen, so a new category came into being that contained only Audrey Hepburn. To the general persona of the gamine, or waif, Hepburn added intelligence, elegance, and an air of "good manners". M. Rosen, in the thoughtful book *Popcorn Venus,* has summed up the Hepburn mystique: "The waif, as portrayed by Audrey Hepburn, provided one of the decade's most intriguing and individualistic heroines. Hepburn simply outdazzled by the sheer force of her piquant *joie de vivre* and the apposite way she was put together. Perhaps it was the unusual combination of a narrow, bony body which she carried like a queen and an elfin face whose doe's eyes contradicted the strength of intelligence in the look, the irregular nose and wide mouth whose smile was at once sensuous, mischievous and absolutely sincere. Then there was her vocal quality, a softened British cadence. Hepburn's presence could elevate the most mundane role because everything about her worked toward a female dignity."

As soon as Hepburn appeared in the public eye, there was a great desire to look like her. In *Movies and Society*, Maurice Jarvie suggests that "One function a star serves is to fix a type of beauty, to help a physical type identify and realize itself. So what happened when Hepburn arrived as a star was that many girls at all resembling her took the hint and set out to exploit those features of themselves that she does. To this end they marshal clothes setting off their slim figures, crop the hair, and use eye make-up for the dewy effect. Again: men now look for and at girls who resemble Hepburn; she crystallized and popularized the sex appeal of a certain type." And it wasn't only star-stuck teenagers who admired and tried to emulate the Hepburn type; according to her biographer, diva Maria Callas chose Hepburn as her model in transforming herself into the svelte and attractive woman she became in mid-career.

Although Hepburn's career is just barely thirty years from its start, it is not too early to say that some of her characterizations will remain forever memorable. Holly Golightly having breakfast outside the windows of Tiffany's; Jo wistfully singing "How Long Has This Been Going On?" in *Funny Face*; Regina's terrified face peering out of the prompt box in the last chase in *Charade*; Natasha in *War and Peace* excitedly telling her mother about the proposal she has received; Eliza Doolittle resplendent at the ball. These images have already proved indelible.

THE EARLY YEARS

n many of her early movies, Audrey Hepburn projects a vulnerable image of a wide-eyed waif, who hopes that by being a good child, always on her best behavior, she will disarm the world and escape the cruel fate so often dealt out to the young and the innocent.

Her childhood suggests she may have had a natural affinity for this role.

Hepburn was born on May 4, 1929, on an estate outside the Belgian city of Brussels. Her mother was a Dutch baroness, born Ella van Heemstra. Audrey's grandfather was a former Governor of the Dutch colony of Surinam, and other members of the family were attached to the royal court. The wealthy van Heemstras owned many properties, including the Castle of Doorn, where the defeated German Kaiser Wilhelm spent his declining years after the end of World War I. It was, in fact, the existence of these properties that caused Audrey's mother to meet her father, the Anglo-Irish banker (some say adventurer) J.A. Hepburn-Ruston. He was the manager of the Brussels branch of the English bank that handled the properties and financial affairs of the van Heemstra family. It would be a second marriage for Audrey's mother, who had already married and divorced a Dutchman, by whom she had two sons.

Audrey's early childhood was passed in comfortable circumstances on an estate with lots of servants, pets, and space to run and play with her half-brothers. But she remembers herself spending many hours alone — a skinny quiet girl who indulged in a lot of make-believe. One guesses there was a fair amount of tension in the family, because Audrey's parents divorced when she was six, apparently as a result of continued disagreement about the way the van Heemstra properties were being handled.

After the divorce, Audrey's mother resumed her maiden name and went home to Holland, while her father returned to England. It was agreed that the Baroness would have custody of the child but that she would attend a boarding school in England so her father would be able to see her regularly. As it turned out, he promptly joined Sir Oswald Mosley's Fascist organization, the Black Shirts, and eventually became totally estranged from his child.

Many of Audrey Hepburn's early publicity photos emphasized her youth and a kind of innocent flirtatiousness.

Six is a tender age to go away to school. Although Audrey spoke English fluently, she must have felt lonely, and far away from all that was secure and familiar. She later commented cryptically, "I was terrified at first about being away from home, but it turned out to be a good lesson in independence." She was still an English schoolgirl, visiting her mother during the summer holidays of 1939, when England declared war on Germany. The Baroness concluded she would be safer in neutral Holland, so Audrey was enrolled in school in Arnhem, where the van Heemstra family had a large estate. That fall, her mother took her to Amsterdam to see a performance by the Sadler's Wells Ballet, and Audrey was captivated. The Baroness, whose early ambition to become an opera singer had been discouraged because it was not a proper activity for a young girl of good family, encouraged Audrey in her ambitions and signed her up for dance lessons at the Arnhem Conservatory with the aging Russian ballerina, Winja Marova.

But the war suddenly engulfed Holland, as the Germans occupied the country. Audrey's mother's brother, a lawyer in Arnhem, was seized as a hostage and executed in retaliation for a plot to blow up a German train. Her cousin, a member of Queen Juliana's court, was also executed. One of her brothers was interned in a labor camp near Berlin. Most of the family estates were confiscated. Audrey herself was once rounded up with a group of other women to be sent to work in a German military kitchen, but she managed to make her escape. She stopped speaking English, called herself Edda van Heemstra, and tried to avoid attracting attention.

But she didn't give up her dancing. She appeared in programs both at the Conservatory and in certain private homes — small gatherings which had a double purpose: to raise money for the Underground and, as Hepburn put it, "frankly, to take our minds from unpleasant things." Her audiences were appreciative but silent, since such gatherings were banned by the German conquerors. There are rumours that Hepburn occasionally gave the Underground more active help, by carrying messages and running errands. She declines to volunteer any concrete information, saying, "Interviewers try to bring it up so often, but it's painful to think about. It was a long time ago, and I'm sure other people have been through much worse. I dislike talking about it because I feel it's not something that should be linked to publicity . . . just the same, mingled in all the nightmares I've had are the war and the cold clutch of human terror."

As the war years passed, the van Heemstra family's problems grew more severe. There was little money and often almost no food. According to Audrey, "We ate nettles, and everyone tried to cook grass, only I couldn't stand it"; they once lived for weeks on nothing but endive. Then Arnhem was bombed and their home was destroyed. They went to live in another of the family estates but were forced to spend most of the day in the cellar, with no heat and little light, because of the intense bombing.

In May of 1945, Arnhem was at last liberated by the British soldiers under Montgomery's command. Hepburn reminisces, "That was the day I learned that freedom has a bouquet, a perfume all its own — that smell of English tobacco and petrol." On a less happy note, she also remembers, "When

First steps in Audrey Hepburn's road to stage fame

were taken in 1952 when she took ballet lessons in

Holland during the war. Short food rations forced

her to give up dancing temporarily.

the British liberated us, I was sixteen years old. I was 5'7" and I weighed 90 pounds, and my ankles and joints were filled with water. I was just a stick."

The war was over, but things remained difficult for Audrey and her mother. Money was still scarce, and so the Baroness was forced to go to work as a cook-housekeeper for a wealthy family in Amsterdam. Young Audrey continued to take ballet lessons, and she also got a chance to make a brief appearance in a short film, *Nederlands In Zeven Lessen (Dutch at the Double)* which was produced, directed and scripted by Hugenot van der Linden and H.M. Josephson; she played an air-hostess in this 48-minute film. In 1948, the year the film was made (Hepburn was 19) she was able to go to London to continue her studies at the highly-regarded studio of Madame Marie Rambert, in Notting Hill Gate.

Madame Rambert recalls of her famous pupil, "She was a wonderful learner. If she had wanted to persevere, she might have become an outstanding ballerina." But Hepburn herself was not so confident that she really had a future as a dancer. She worried about her height and also her big feet. She later commented, "I wanted to be a ballet dancer, but I was too tall. I tried everything to make it an asset. Instead of working on *allegro* – little small tight movements – I took extra courses in *adagio*, so that I could use my long lines to advantage. I made the most of my long legs and long back, to have people say she's tall because she has long lines instead of having them say she's too tall to be a dancer."

Moreover, she realized that the financial aspect of the long training she would need presented real problems in view of the continued difficulties of the van Heemstra family. "I would have needed five more years of training. I hadn't a penny to my name. I couldn't have gone in the chorus earning five pounds a week, out of which I had to pay for my tights, shoes, rent, and food." After ten years of austerity, it is not surprising that the twenty-year-old girl found the prospect of many more years of sacrifice unattractive .

So Hepburn decided to find another way to use her assets of good looks, a lithe body, and a remarkably poised manner. Before she had been in London a year, she had found work (one of the ten chosen out of a total of 3000 applicants) as a chorus girl in the musical *High Button Shoes*, at a salary of £8 a week. "I wanted to be a dancer, but rather than slave away at something I felt I'd lose by in the end, I went into *High Button Shoes*. It did for exactly what I needed. I was in a show with music – twelve times a week. I needed music in my life very badly. Then I was in a dressing room with other girls. That brought me back to normal. It was the joy of living that enabled me to work."

The next year found her on the stage again, in the Cambridge Theatre's revue, *Sauce Tartare,* produced by Cecil Landau. She continued to work very hard, trying to make her way in her new profession. She appeared in Ciro's nightclub after the curtain went down on the revue. She posed for an advertisement for Lacto-Calomine, a complexion lotion. She also did some fashion modelling, using her spare figure and long legs to great advantage in elegant clothes; this was the period when she first met Hubert de

As a dancer, Hepburn's principal strength was the long fluid line she exhibits here.

MP
1353

Givenchy, the *couturier* whose work in the late 1950s and early '60s was so intertwined with Hepburn's own personal image. And Hepburn also began to take acting lessons, obviously with an eye to moving out of the chorus and into larger speaking parts. Her teacher was Felix Aylmer; among his earlier students had been Charles Laughton. She says of Aylmer, "He taught me to concentrate intelligently on what I was doing."

In 1950, Hepburn was cast in Landau's new revue, *Sauce Piquante*, and she had the chance to emerge momentarily from the chorus for a short solo. That brief moment in the spotlight was a turning point; it gave her that first chance to be noticed. And she was: director Mario Zampi, in London to begin a new film for Associated British Pictures Corporation, saw her on stage (he claims he went back thirteen more times because of her!) and picked her to play a nightclub girl in a tiny scene. The legend goes that when he got her in the studio and saw how well she could flutter her lashes in silent flirtation, he doubled the size of her part and allowed her to stay on the screen for all of 20 seconds! The movie was *Laughter in Paradise*, a comedy about the various relatives of a rich man with an ironical turn of mind, who try to live up to the stringent terms of his final bequest. Among the excellent cast were Hugh Griffith, Alastair Sim, Kay Compton, Guy Middleton, and Joyce Grenfell.

That appearance (and Zampi's enthusiasm) led to a contract in 1950 for Hepburn with Associated British. Soon they found other bit parts for their young contract player. She got three days work in *One Wild Oat*, a film version by Eros-Coronet of a very successful stage farce. She was an unbilled extra in this picture which, like *Laughter in Paradise*, was released in 1951; it starred Robertson Hare, Stanley Holloway, June Sylvaine, and Andrew Crawford. She also appeared momentarily in the classic comedy, *The Lavender Hill Mob*. Directed by Charles Crichton, this wonderful film starred Alec Guinness as a scheming bank clerk turned thief; supporting him were Stanley Holloway, Sidney James, Alfie Bass, and Marjorie Fielding as a sublimely oblivious landlandy. Hepburn fans who watch closely will recognized her as the girl in the South American sequence with Alec Guinness at the very end of the film.

The fourth picture made in 1950 and released in 1951 that provided a bit part for Hepburn was *Young Wives' Tale*, another play turned into a movie, under the direction of Henry Cass. This time her part was a fraction larger: she played a man-hunting girl who takes a room in a house shared by two couples and promptly falls in love with one of the husbands, causing momentary difficulties in the marriage. The film, which starred Joan Greenwood and Nigel Patrick, saw only limited release in the US when it was first issued, but it was re-released several years later (1952) to capitalize on Hepburn's new-found stardom. Bosley Crowther called it "a dismal situation comedy . . . leaked from an uninspired brain," but commended "that pretty Audrey Hepburn."

The next year, 1951, was a critical year in Hepburn's life. She began it by working in a film called *The Secret People*. Its director, Thorold Dickinson, had (like Mario Zampi) seen and liked Hepburn in *Sauce Piquante*,

At the beginning of her screen career, Hepburn had not yet learned to use eyeliner and to deliberately thicken her eyebrows in order to balance the width of her mouth.

and had in fact tested her at that time for a part in a movie he was planning. But he had difficulties in assembling the rest of his cast, and it was not until several years later that he was at last ready to shoot the film — and offer Hepburn a part. *The Secret People* was a complicated drama about a glamorous refugee (Valentina Cortesa) who is blackmailed into participating in an assassination plot. When the plot fails, killing instead an innocent bystander, she cooperates with the police in bringing the plotters to justice. Hepburn plays Cortesa's younger sister Nora, and for the first time she is really recognizably the young woman who became a star. Nora is an idealistic young dance student — loving, impetuous, eager. Her long dark hair hangs down her back, her eyes (without their usual heavy makeup) seem open and trusting. The voice is already fully characteristic, with its odd combination of primness and sensuality, and the slightly mannered intonation. *Secret People* provides us with the one remaining glimpse of Hepburn as a real working dancer, in a scene in which she auditions for a job with a ballet company. Her quick steps are a bit awkward, and occasionally her balance seems tenuous, but her line is long and smooth, and the movements of her arms and head are unfailingly graceful. In reviewing the film, *Variety* called it "a dull and rather confused offering" but raved that "Audrey Hepburn combines beauty with skill, shining particularly in two short dance sequences."

Before *The Secret People* was released, Hepburn was tested by MGM (at the suggestion of Alec Guinness) for a big part in *Quo Vadis*. But they gave the part to better-known Deborah Kerr instead. Then, at the urging of Associated British, director William Wyler agreed to test Hepburn as a long-shot candidate for the lead in his forthcoming *Roman Holiday*. Both he and the studio execs at Paramount wanted Jean Simmons for this role, but the negotiations to borrow her from Howard Hughes were stalled. So Wyler agreed to having a test made in England. Although the test impressed a number of people, Hepburn was still not considered a serious possibility to carry a major motion picture, and Paramount continued to pursue Jean Simmons. They thought they might find something else in future that would be a suitable property for Hepburn.

◁ Audrey in jaunty nautical costume in 1952.

▷ The curly hair, the clunky earrings were soon to be eliminated from the "Hepburn look"; this is a publicity still from *Young Wives Tale*.

Although Associated British was having no luck in the attempt to turn Hepburn into a major star, they managed to keep her working. They suggested her for a part in a British/French production called *Monte Carlo Baby*. It was to be shot on location on the Riviera, first in one language, then in the other. There was a small supporting role that seemed right for Hepburn.

She remembers very clearly how it happened. "The day the producer interviewed me was one of those days when *everything* went wrong. I had a terrible time finding a stocking that didn't have a run in it. The zipper got caught in my dress. And when I finally arrived at my agent's office, the whole interview lasted exactly a minute and a half! I was sure I'd failed. I tried to comfort myself by telling Mother that if I went to Monte Carlo for this small part, I might miss out on a larger role in London. And anyway, someday I'd make enough money so that we both could go to the Riviera on *my* expense account. Then suddenly the phone rang and I heard those four words that are the sweetest music to every actress, 'The job is yours.'"

Her first shooting on location brought with it a separation from the man she had been seeing regularly. He was James Hanson, a young and good-looking executive of a transportation company, and his intentions were obviously serious; they announced their engagement just before she left. But at that moment, her career came first, so she packed her bags for Monte Carlo.

Monte Carlo Baby was really a succession of skits linked together by the intermittent appearance of bandleader Ray Ventura and his orchestra. It was directed by Jean Boyer and Jean Jerrold, and starred Jules Munshin, Michelle Framer, Cara Williams, and Philippe LeMaire. Hepburn plays a film star, married to but estranged from a concert pianist (John Van Dreeland). Their child is in a sort of daycare center that is suddenly closed by an attack of measles. Hepburn's child is mistakenly delivered to a touring musician (Russell Collins) with much consternation to all parties involved. This movie was released in England and in France in 1953, but there was no interest in US distribution until after Hepburn had become a star. Then US producers Collier Young and Ida Lupino bought the rights and showed it to rather confused American audiences who could not understand why a star was next appearing as a supporting player.

The most important thing that happened to Audrey Hepburn in Monte Carlo was only tangentially related to the film. She was standing by as the crew set up the kleig lights and prepared to shoot a brief scene that showed her emerging from the front door of the Hotel de Paris, a radiant bride on her honeymoon. One of the spectators of this little scene, as it was blocked out and rehearsed, was herself a guest at the hotel. It was the famous French writer Colette, by this time an arthritic old lady confined to her wheelchair, but unmistakeably a formidable presence. She watched young Hepburn move, smile, talk; then she turned to her husband and exclaimed triumphantly, "Voila! There is my Gigi!"

This publicity photo shows the beginning of Audrey

Hepburn's new look for the Sixties. Her hair is sleek,

her earrings are small buttons, her blouse is simply

cut with no collar at all.

Launching a Career

At seventy-eight years of age, Colette, with a simple glance and the right word, caused a new star to rise in the theatrical firmament." Colette herself was amazed by the coincidence of her discovery. "What author ever expects to see one of his brain-children appear suddenly in the flesh? Not I, and yet, here it was. This unknown young woman . . . was my own thoroughly French Gigi come alive!"

Gigi, the last of Colette's works of fiction, was written in the dark days of the German occupation of Paris. Perhaps to distract herself from the worries of the present, Colette returned in her imagination to the past, when she herself was only a few years older than her heroine — back to the turn of the century, the days of the great courtesans, elaborately choreographed social relationships, and a fashionable world that appreciated both

This is Hepburn's moment, as a cigarette girl in *Laughter in Paradise*; the combination of the saucy costume and the innocent face captivated several directors.

luxury and gaiety. Her coltish heroine is a fifteen-and-a-half-year-old school-girl who not only manages to captivate one of the most dashing bachelors of the day, but in an improbably happy ending, to marry him as well. The novelette is full of charming period details about clothes, jewelry, manners, and the games of romance. When it was published in 1945, it was just what war-weary Europeans were waiting to read, and it was an immediate and enormous success.

Gigi was made into a frothy French movie in 1948, and that in turn led to the idea of a stage version for Broadway. Famed producer Gilbert Miller bought the rights and then hired Anita Loos (author of *Gentlemen Prefer Blondes*) to adapt the book for the American theater. All was going well by the summer of 1951, except for one major snag: no one could find the right girl to play Gigi. Loos recalls, "Finding just the right actress for the role of Gigi was a difficult job because the part ran the entire gamut of female emotions, but the girl who played it must not look more than 15 years old. Colette was reasonably certain that she had stumbled upon the star for her story, although the girl never had spoken a word on the stage."

Colette cabled Miller in London and told him to look up her discovery as soon as Hepburn returned from Monte Carlo. He did, and in turn immediately telephoned Loos in New York, telling her to hurry over to London to see for herself. Loos was about to leave for a holiday in Paris with a friend, actress Paulette Goddard, but they agreed to alter their plans and head for London first. According to Loos, "We were in our suite at the Savoy Hotel when Colette's discovery was announced. The girl came in, dressed in a simple white shirtwaist and skirt, but Paulette and I were bowled over by her unusual type of beauty. After talking a moment, we arranged an audition for her to read for Gilbert the following day. But after she left, Paulette said to me, 'There's got to be something wrong with that girl!' I asked, 'What?' 'Anyone who looks like that would have been discovered before she was ten years old. Something's radically wrong with her.'"

Despite this rather odd suspicion, Miller signed Hepburn to play the part of Gigi. He later commented cheerfully on the riskiness of giving the part to "a young actress whom we had never seen on a stage, indeed, a young actress whose two years stage experience had been confined to dancing bits in topical revues."

Before Hepburn left London, there was another milestone in her career. When Paramount production head Don Hartman heard that she was going to star on Broadway, and remembered the favorable impression her screen test had caused, he decided that he'd better move quickly. So at his instructions the head of Paramount in London, Richard Mealand, offered her a contract. At that time, Paramount still had no specific picture in mind for her.

Hepburn sailed to New York to begin rehearsals for *Gigi* in the middle of September, 1951. Loos recalls that Audrey was so tempted by the delicious food on the luxury liner, after the privations of war-time Holland and post-war England; that she gained 15 pounds before she arrived in New York! "When Gilbert saw her, he was appalled. He had engaged a sprite, who had suddenly turned into a dumpling. Gilbert, as a gourmand,

Audrey Hepburn's big scene in *The Secret People*

came when Nora auditioned for a role in a dance

performance. Her sister, played by Valentina

Cortesa, watches by the piano with her fingers

crossed

couldn't believe that his Gigi would ever get down to weight. Rehearsals began with Gilbert regarding his ingenue's weight with a skeptical eye. But Mortie (Miller's second-in-command) put Audrey on a diet of steak tartare at Dinty Moore's next door to our 46th Street theater. Her pounds slowly began to melt, and to date, they have never returned."

Hepburn herself had some misgivings about her sudden big break. She later told an interviewer, "When Colette proposed it, I replied that I wasn't equipped to play a leading role since I'd never said more than one or two lines on the stage. But she said, 'You've been a dancer, you've worked hard, and you can work hard and do this too.' Her conviction encouraged me and when I returned to London I signed a contract with Mr. Miller." On the same theme, she also told *Time* magazine, "I tried to explain to all of them that I wasn't ready to do a lead, but they didn't agree, and I certainly wasn't going to argue with them."

This was not false modesty; it was a genuine recognition on her part that being an actress requires more than simply decorating the stage. In the weeks of rehearsals and previews, she often worked as much as 21 hours a day, trying to learn her craft. "I decided to be an actress. And I knew right then and there I'd just have to pull up my socks and live up to what was expected of me." It *was* hard work. Anita Loos recalls that they were all worried about the demands of such a difficult role for an inexperienced actress. For example, "In rehearsing Gigi's passionate blowup at the climax of the last act, Audrey remained much more the petulant teenager than a young woman suffering the sharp anguish of a first tragic love affair." Veteran actress Cathleen Nesbitt, who played Gigi's aunt in the play, has said, "She was terribly frightened. She didn't have much idea of phrasing. She had no idea how to project, and she would come bounding onto the stage like a gazelle. But she had that rare thing – audience authority, the thing that makes everybody look at you when you are on the stage."

Gigi opened at the Fulton Theater on Saturday night, November 24, 1951. In addition to Hepburn and Nesbitt, the cast included Josephine Brown as Gigi's grandmother; Doris Patson as her mother; Michael Evans as the rich and dashing Gaston Lachaille, who marries Gigi in the end; and Bertha Belmore and Francis Compton as knowing servants. When Hepburn walked off the stage at the end of the performance, the stage manager told her, "I don't know how you're going to get inside your dressing room. It's full of flowers." It was also full of celebrities, among them Helen Hayes and Marlene Dietrich. Most definitely, a star was born that night.

Most of the reviews were lukewarm about the play (and Loos' writing in particular) but greatly admiring of Hepburn's performance. Brooks Atkinson called her "a young actress of charm, honesty and talent who ought to be interned in America and trapped into appearing in a fine play . . . As Gigi, she develops a full-length character from artless gaucheries in the first act to a stirring emotional climax in the last scene (That was the one that so worried Loos in rehearsal.) It is a fine piece of sustained acting that is spontaneous, lucid, captivating." *Variety* called her "a real find, with looks, figure, talent, authority and above all, personal magnetism . . . The actress has an effective light touch, but she can make a dramatic point when the

△ It was the French novelist Colette who spotted Audrey Hepburn and insisted she should have the title role in the Broadway production of *Gigi*.

▷ During the period when Audrey Hepburn was engaged to James Hanson, they were frequently seen and photographed out on the town.

script requires it, and has the authority and personality to dominate a scene. considering her comparatively limited experience on the legit stage, she has impressive range and presence." Critic Walter Kerr said, "Miss Hepburn is as fresh and frisky as a puppy out of a tub. She brings a candid innocence and a tomboy intelligence to a part that might have gone sticky, and her perform-ance comes as a breath of fresh air in a stifling season . . . She is expressive and touching in a silent scene as she hears her aunt bargaining away her future favors, and at the end of the play, when she treats her horror-stricken family to a heretical defense of marriage, she has all the authority and fire needed to carry the day."

After reading the glowing reviews, Gilbert Miller promised to put Hepburn's name up in lights. By the end of the week, it was blazing on the Fulton Theater marquee — and Hepburn got to screw in the final bulb for luck. According to the oft-told story, her comment was, "Oh, dear, and I still have to learn to act."

Hepburn was cooperative with the press. She posed for pub-licity pictures wearing the latest hats at Macy's, gave interviews, and endlessly told the story of her discovery by Colette. But she continued to lead a quiet life, with a schedule that revolved almost entirely around the demands of her work. She took a small suite in a hotel and customarily went to bed right after the curtain went down. Her fiancé came to New York and gave her a diamond engagement ring, then moved to Toronto, where he had a branch office; she saw him on occasional weekends. She stayed out of nightclubs and didn't drink. Most people who knew her agreed that Hepburn at 22 retained the air of a *jeune fille*. Her only vice seemed to be her taste for great quantities of rare meat (perhaps an addiction caused by that diet of steak tartare?) An interviewer for the *New York World Telegram* reported on going out to lunch with her. "'Look,' she'll say to a waitress, 'the tenderloin steak please, but very rare. You know what I mean? Raw rare. With the blood in it. Dripping. Very rare. Almost raw.' Generally the waitress gets the idea. Some of the meat Audrey eats is rare enough to have walked into the restaurant five minutes before."

Paramount executive Don Hartman went to see Hepburn in *Gigi* several times and then returned to Hollywood and reran her screen test. Canny William Wyler had told the English test director to keep on filming after calling "Cut". "'She was absolutely delightful,' recalled Wyler. "First she played the scene from the script, then you heard someone yell 'Cut' but the take continued. She jumped up in bed, relaxed now, and asked 'How was it? Was I any good?' She looked and saw that everybody was so quiet and that the lights were still on. Suddenly she realized that the camera was still running and we got *that* reaction too. Acting, looks, and personality . . . The test became sort of famous and was once shown on TV."

Since Jean Simmons was still unavailable, Hartman and Wyler began to consider the possibility of using Hepburn as the star of *Roman Holiday*. Wyler said, "I wanted a girl without an American accent to play the princess, someone you could *believe* was brought up a princess." In a matter of weeks, Hepburn was signed, at a salary of $12,500, to star in the film. The only problem was when she would be able to do it. *Gigi* showed every sign of

Here she is on the set of her first starring film, *Roman Holiday* with leading man Gregory Peck. Her look is quintessential Fifties: short tousled hair, turned-up collar, wide belt, voluminous skirt.

turning into a long-run success, and Wyler was ready to start shooting his $3 million picture. Finally, an agreement with Gilbert Miller was worked out. The Broadway show would close at the beginning of the summer, and all of Hepburn's scenes would be shot before she had to report back to begin the road tour in September. The rest of the picture would be shot around her.

Such a tight schedule made the relatively unknown Hepburn an even bigger gamble, but Wyler and Paramount stuck to their decision. The day after *Gigi* closed in New York, Hepburn boarded a plane for Rome, where the film was being shot on location. The next day, she was at work in her role as Princess Anne.

Roman Holiday was originally conceived by Frank Capra (although many other writers worked on it later.) He had noticed a picture in the newspaper taken by a snooping photographer with a telephoto lens, of Princess Margaret in a white bathing suit on holiday in Capri. He quickly conjured up a little fairy tale about a beautiful young princess, trapped in the confines of royal protocol, who manages to escape for 24 hours and blissfully enjoy doing just as she pleases. A handsome American newspaperman (Gregory Peck) finds her half-asleep on a park bench and takes her home to his apartment without knowing who she is. When he discovers her true identity, he stays with her and shows her around Rome, hoping to get the scoop of his career. They fall a little bit in love, but in the end, the Princess goes dutifully back to her gilded cage and the reporter tears up the story.

Certain aspects of the plot are reminiscent of Capra's earlier hit, *It Happened One Night*, with its incognito heiress and cynical hero with an ulterior motive that evaporates under the pressures of love. Even certain scenes are similar: for example, in Peck's difficulties in choosing the proper sleeping arrangements for a visiting princess there is a decided echo of the famous motel bedroom scene with Claudette Colbert and Clark Gable finally separated by a hanging blanket. But in Wyler's hands, the story has an entirely different tone. It's no longer the screwball comedy of the Thirties but the escapist sentimentalism of the Fifties. We smile at many of the scenes — the weary princess slipping off her shoes underneath her voluminuous gown, the happy abandon with which she eats an ice cream cone — but we don't laugh. And instead of the comic wedding that is the climax of *It Happened One Night*, we have a bitter-sweet renunciation that brings tears to the more susceptible members of the audience.

Much that was effective about Hepburn's screen image was crystallized in *Roman Holiday*. She told reporters on the first day of filming that she was grateful to have a chance to do a film with Wyler so early in her career, and so she should have been. He saw what she had, and was able to make it appear on the screen. As one critic later put it, "Wyler undoubtedly helped her create the persona for which she is best-known: the tomboy-elf, the fey gamine, dreamy and strong, capable of exciting highs and depressing lows . . ." The combination of the story line and Wyler's direction emphasized her child-woman quality, and her role as princess/prisoner was the first in a long line of Hepburn heroines who are for various blameless reasons incapable of dealing competently with the ordinary world.

Taken in 1953 shortly after winning the Oscar for Best

Actress of the Year for her performance in *Roman*

Holiday.

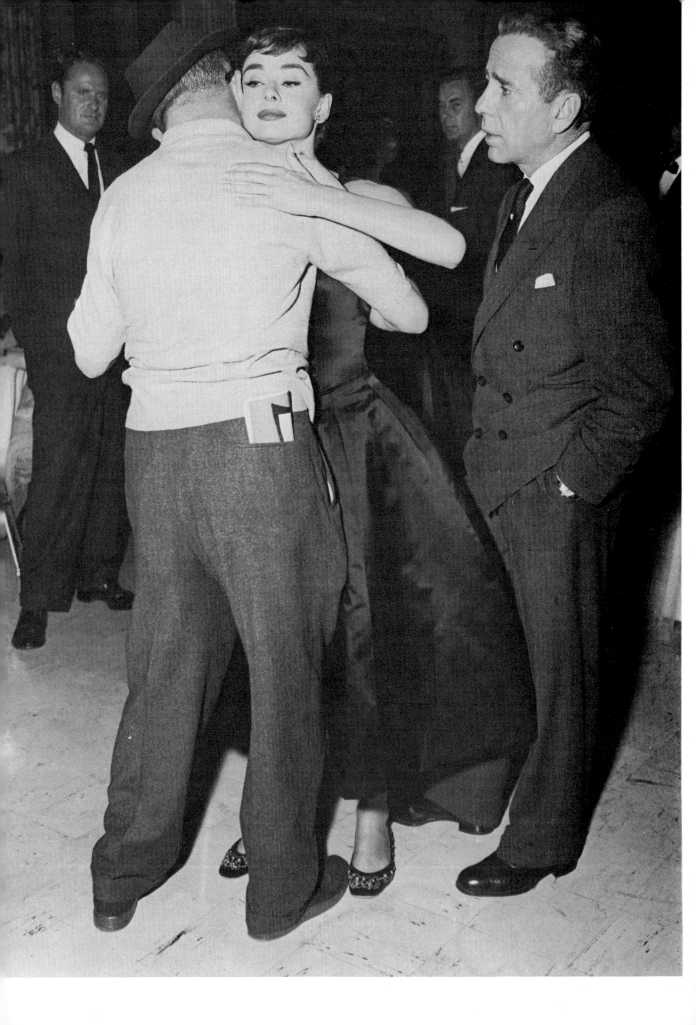

The set of *Roman Holiday* seems to have been an unusually happy one, despite the pressures of the schedule. Certainly the compliments flowed. Hepburn said, "Gregory Peck always put me at ease before starting a scene. He's very professional and thorough when it comes to work . . . I soon learned to relax, to look for guidance from Peck and William Wyler. I trusted them and they never let me down." Don Hartman said of Hepburn, "She couldn't be more conscientious. She's a wonderful, wonderful girl." Wyler extolled Peck's relaxed charm, and wryly told an interviewer, "Peck used to a somber sort of fellow. In *Roman Holiday,* he simply learned to put his hands in his pockets." Of Hepburn, he said flatly, "That girl is going to be the biggest star in Hollywood."

In September, Hepburn flew back to New York for brief rehearsals before *Gigi* went out on the road. Wyler finished shooting the rest of the film and then did all the postproduction work in Rome. Hartman flew over to see an early cut (three hours and 20 minutes long at that point.) He remembers being in a freezing projection room. "There was a stove at my feet. I was wearing an overcoat, a hat and a muffler. I never saw a picture under more uncomfortable circumstances." But when the screening was over, he sent a cable to Paramount's top execs, Barney Balaban and Y. Frank Freeman: "In my opinion we have the greatest comedy since *It Happened One Night.* Audrey Hepburn will be the greatest star in Hollywood."

Paramount gave the movie a big première in London in August of 1953. The location was chosen in part to emphasize the parallel between the movie's Princess Anne and England's Princess Margaret, whose romance with Peter Townsend was then a hot item in the media. Of course, the studio loudly denied that there was any resemblance, but there's no doubt the "coincidence" helped make audiences believe in the film's fairy tale.

It was immediately clear that *Roman Holiday* was going to be a big success. Within a few weeks of its release, *Time* made the movie the subject of a cover story, and there was also extensive coverage in *Life* and *Look.* It did big box office business; the film grossed more than $7 million in its first year, which is a lot of tickets in those days of cheap admission prices.

And the reviews were uniformly good — especially for Audrey Hepburn. The *New York Times* said, "She is a slender, elfin, and wistful beauty, alternately regal and childlike in her profound appreciation of the newly-found simple pleasures and love." The *Herald Tribune* critic called her "a remarkable young actress who carries off the finale with a nicety that leaves one a little haunted." *Time* raved, "Exquisitely blending queenly dignity and bubbling mischief, a stick-slim actress with huge, limpid eyes and a heart-shaped face was teaching US moviegoers last week a lesson they already knew and loved — that the life of a princess is not a happy one . . . Audrey Hepburn's princess never seems to forget her exalted station, even when she is gulping an ice cream cone, getting her hair cut or whamming a cop over the head with a guitar in a nightclub dustup. Yet to scenes where she is playing the princess proper, she brings a wistfulness that seems completely unposed. She can be infinitely appealing with her hair snarled and her dress dripping wet. In the film's final moments, she becomes a lonely little figure of great pathos and dignity."

On the set of Sabrina, Billy Wilder demonstrates how

Humphrey Bogart should dance with Audrey Hep-

burn; Bogart looks understandably wary.

The film still holds up today, but of course we now see it in a somewhat different light. Thirty years later, it seems most remarkable for its old-fashioned quality. It belongs with the older "Ruritanian romances", such as the archetypal *Merry Widow* or even the Betty Grable film of the Forties, *That Lady in Ermine*. It looks backward, in contrast to other well-remembered films of the Fifties, such as *East of Eden* or *A Place in the Sun* that look forward to the new realism.

There have been recent suggestions that the film is really about a woman trying to break out of societal constraints; M.A. Anderegg comments, "Both as a princess and as a woman, Anne must wear uncomfortable clothes, must behave with strict decorum, must say only what she has been prompted to say." The film can also be read as a fable about the conflict between love and duty, in which case the moral is that women must put duty (to society) above personal happiness. Another way to look at it is in terms of the fact that the princess, next in line for the throne, is about to take on a masculine role, that of governing a kingdom; therefore she must renounce her femininity – in this instance, her desire for love – in order to be worthy.

It is surely a significant part of Hepburn's screen persona that her character can only reach out for happiness through the traditional child's solution of running away from home. One cannot imagine her taking the adult step of confronting the ministers and courtiers (the grownups in her world) and demanding that she be allowed the freedom she wants. It is even more difficult to imagine the Hepburn child-woman throwing everything over for passion. Perhaps it was this very lack of sexuality at the core of the movie that permitted the audience to take it as a fairy tale and enjoy its sentimentality without being disturbed by any whiff of deep-seated emotion.

With the almost instantaneous success of *Roman Holiday*, things began to move even more quickly for Audrey Hepburn. Paramount lined up her next picture, *Sabrina*, most of which was to be shot in the Hollywood studio, right away. Before she went out to the coast, she took the major step of breaking her engagement to James Hansen – despite the fact that she had already bought a wedding dress and ordered the invitations. She explained, "When I found out that I didn't even have time to attend to the furnishing of our London flat, I suddenly knew that I would make a pretty bad wife. I would forever have to be studying parts, fitting costumes, and giving interviews. What a humiliating spot to put my husband in . . . making him stand by holding my coat while I signed autographs." At least for the time being, her career came first. As she acknowledged on another occasion, ". . . it would be impossible for me to give up my career completely. I just can't. I've worked too long to achieve something. And so many people have helped me along the way, I don't want to let them down."

So she went out to Los Angeles, moved into a modest apartment on Wilshire Boulevard (with two poodles) and began to work on *Sabrina*. Its director was Billy Wilder, another of Hollywood's top-ranked directors. The movie was based on a witty Broadway play called *Sabrina Fair*, which starred Margaret Sullavan. It was written by Samuel Taylor, who is also listed as a collaborator on the screenplay, but most of the movie version was written

The Hepburn look for *Sabrina*.

AUDREY HEPBURN

by Ernest Lehman and Wilder himself. Hepburn plays Sabrina, the beautiful young daughter of a wealthy family's chauffeur (John Williams), who grows up over the garage of their Long Island estate and falls in love with the dashing playboy son of the family (William Holden with platinumized hair.) When she realizes he doesn't even notice her, the naive young girl attempts suicide, and her distressed father responds by packing her off to Paris — ostensibly to learn gourmet cooking but really to turn herself into a glamorous and sophisticated charmer. When she returns in her new incarnation, Holden finally takes notice of her, so much so that his parents concoct a scheme to save him from her clutches. Part of the plot calls for the stuffy elder son of the family (Humphrey Bogart) to pretend to court Sabrina. Predictably, he himself ends up falling in love with her, and eventually sweeps her off her feet.

Wilder always worked by picking his stars first and then building the script around them; as he put it, "What good is it to have a magnificent dramatic concept for Sir Laurence Olivier and Audrey Hepburn if they're not available?" Hepburn was his one and only choice for Sabrina. He told a reporter, "After so many drive-in waitresses in movies — it's been a real drought — here is class, somebody who went to school, can spell and possibly play the piano. She's like a salmon swimming upstream. And she can do it with very small bazooms. Titism has taken over the country. This girl single-handed may make bazooms a thing of the past. The director will not have to invent shots where the girl leans forward for a glass of Scotch and soda. Not since Garbo has there been anything like her, with the possible exception of Bergman."

Wilder's original choice for the older brother had been Cary Grant, who backed out at the last minute. Humphrey Bogart was an inspired piece of casting (and he was to get the best reviews from the critics) but it called for extensive rewriting to make the script fit him. Worse yet, it was clear from the first week on the set that Wilder and Bogart were not getting along (an understatement.) Someone who knew them both well explained, "Bogart was a man of caprices, which Billy did not find amusing. Bogart thought that a director must humble himself before Bogart. On a Billy Wilder picture, there is no star but Billy."

Their antagonism created ugly scenes on the set and created an atmosphere of real tension for all concerned; Hepburn must have found it a far cry from the happy family feeling that pervaded the set of *Roman Holiday*. Wilder blamed Bogart for never studying his lines; Bogart retorted that all the dialogue seemed to be written only the night before the scene was shot. The situation was at its worst near the end of the shooting. According to Wilder's biographer, Maurice Zolotow, "Rumors — probably started by Wilder — began circulating around the set. Lehman and Wilder were going to write it so that Audrey Hepburn would fall into the arms of Holden. Bogart went around muttering, 'I'm gonna get fucked . . . I'm not gonna get the girl . . . Billy's going to throw it to his buddy Holden . . .' This was Wilder's most effective thrust. He deliberately kept Bogart in suspense, torturing him, until the last few days of filming."

A youthful Audrey with Renee Heimer, Jean

Simmons's stand-in before she went to Hollywood.

Throughout it all, Hepburn managed the difficult feat of remaining friends with everyone. The Bogarts had a dinner party for her; William Holden served her tea in his dressing room and said, "I think people love her off the screen for the same reason they love her performances—a kind of orderliness and formality." Wilder gave her a bright green bicycle to ride around the studio and raved, "There is no one like her."

And despite all the undercurrents on the set, the actual shooting progressed quickly, taking only nine weeks in the fall of 1953. (Hepburn was paid $15,000 for her work.) *Sabrina* was released in 1954 and became one of the most successful films of the year. The movie has a slightly odd tone: it's a fairy tale told by a cynic. It opens with the immortal words, "Once upon a time," and is clearly one more version of the Cinderella story. But it has those sharp touches of Wilder's satire — for example, the line, "Nobody poor has ever been called democratic for marrying somebody rich." There is also the Wilder vulgarity, as evidenced in the decidedly unfunny scene in which William Holden sits on a wineglass, with damage to his posterior. As critic Karel Reisz put it, "The subsequent scenes, where the affected region is constantly being prodded and kicked by hearty fellow characters, firmly overstep the narrow dividing line between slapstick and viciousness."

So it was an odd vehicle that Wilder created for Audrey Hepburn — a glass coach that keeps turning into a pumpkin at embarrassing morphoses into a sophisticated woman, with the most elegant wardrobe Hubert de Givenchy could design. This unusual combination of fey innocence and haute couture elegance is uniquely Hepburn's.
ness thrown in along the way. In her second film, *Sabrina*, she continues to display her winning girlishness, but somewhere along the way she metamorphoses into a sophisticated woman, with the most elegant wardrobe Hubert de Givenchy could design. This unusual combination of fey innocence and haute couture elegance is uniquely Hepburn's.

It is not surprising that after Hepburn's sudden rise to stardom, some reviewers would be sharpening their knives; Hepburn herself acknowledged, "It's the second big film which will prove if I was really worthy of the first." Although fans continued to be enthusiastic, critics were somewhat less effusive about her second outing. *Films in Review* hit out, "Needless to say, Miss Hepburn is fey and gaminish about getting her man, and in one sequence is costumed to emphasize her lack of what are technically known as secondary sexual characteristics. In some camera angles, her face, which can be so winsome, is quite ugly, and in *Sabrina* she disenchants as often as she charms. Her voice is not always well used, and some of its best effects are borrowed from Joan Greenwood." *Time's* reviewer was downright cruel: "Actress Hepburn's appeal, it becomes clearer with every appearance, is largely to the imagination; the less acting she does, the more people can imagine her doing, and wisely she does very little in *Sabrina*." However, not everyone took such a dim view of her performance. *Variety* said she "again demonstrates a winning talent for being Miss Cinderella," and the *Christian Science Monitor* said, "Miss Hepburn is principally required to be bewitching, a requirement she fulfills with no trouble at all."

Audrey Hepburn receives the Academy Award for

her 1953 film *Roman Holiday*. This is the period of

what Cecil Beaton called her "rat-nibbled hair";

Hepburn remained remarkably undefensive in the face of the criticism. She told one reporter, "Acting doesn't come easy to me. I put a tremendous amount of effort into every morsel that comes out. I don't yet feel that I have enough experience or store of knowledge to fall back upon." Of course, she could afford to be modest, because acting honors were beginning to pour in. At about the time she finished shooting *Sabrina*, it was announced that Hepburn had been nominated for the Academy Award for *Roman Holiday*. (Other nominees were Deborah Kerr, Leslie Caron, Ava Gardner, and Maggie McNamara.) She was named the Best Actress of the Year by the New York Film Critics Circle, and she also won the British award, the Picturegoer Gold Medal.

All these announcements came as she moved quickly into her next venture, a return to the Broadway stage. She went to New York in December of 1953, taking her mother along for company, to begin rehearsals for *Ondine*. The Jean Giraudoux play was directed by Alfred Lunt and co-starred Mel Ferrer. She had met Ferrer that summer, through Gregory Peck; the two actors were friends and both closely involved with the prestigious LaJolla Theater productions. She saw him occasionally while she was working on the Paramount set, and they both liked the idea of doing a play together. At that point in her career, Hepburn considered herself very much a part of the theater and expressed her determination to continue working on the stage, no matter how successful she might be in films.

It was Ferrer who came up with *Ondine*, which he had seen beautifully staged in Paris. It was a real challenge for Hepburn. She played another fairytale character, a water nymph who falls in love with a mortal knight (Ferrer). But eventually she realizes that he needs the real-world comforts that only another mortal can provide, and so she relinquishes him to her human rival. The dialogue and action are heavily stylized, and the success of the play depends entirely on creating a mood that persuades the audience to believe in the reality of the mythical Ondine. Hepburn worked hard to handle this difficult role. Lunt remarked that he was enormously impressed by her ability to learn and to take direction. There were numerous rumors that he did not feel so warmly about Ferrer's professionalism.

Ondine opened on Broadway in February, 1954; in addition to Hepburn and Ferrer, it starred John Alexander, Alan Hewitt and Marian Seldes. Elliot Norton said of Hepburn, "This Ondine is a spirit of the storm, a child of 16, an alluring young woman – all in one. She is comic and tragic, worldly and other-worldly; elusive, appealing, gay, pathetic." William Becker opined, "I have tried to analyze what it is that Miss Hepburn brings to this role, and I can only conclude that it is something like raw genius . . . She survives and triumphs on a kind of sheer will (and sometimes, wilfulness) an indescribably vital intensity that simply subjects and transforms whatever stands between her and the purest projection of what she feels the role should be." There was some less-high-minded comment about her costume, designed by Valentina: "Miss Hepburn's third act appearance in a fish net secured only by some strategically located seaweed produced unabashed mooning . . ."

In late 1954, Audrey Hepburn marries Mel Ferrer in a quiet little Swiss village.

On March 25, 1954, the Academy Awards ceremonies were held, and Hepburn won the Oscar for Best Actress. In her brief acceptance speech, she simply said that she was grateful to all the people who had helped her. Later she confided, "I was so surprised when they called my name that I didn't know what to do. Mother and I wanted to celebrate, so we bought a bottle of champagne on the way home. It was warm – but it was the best champagne I ever tasted."

Two days later, she had a chance to celebrate all over again, when it was announced that she had won the Tony for her stage performance in *Ondine*. (Only one other actress, Shirley Booth, has ever managed to win both these awards in the same year.) "How will I ever live up to them?" Hepburn asked. "It's like being given something when you're a child, something too big for you that you must grow into."

When the run of *Ondine* was concluded, there was one more reason to celebrate. Audrey Hepburn and Mel Ferrer slipped away to Switzerland to be married in September, 1954.

The Decade of the Fifties

The first thing on the agenda for the new Mrs. Ferrer was a chance to rest and relax. Since the fall of 1951 – for nearly three years – she had been working under great pressure at her acting career without a break. And of course, the years before that, when she was studying and trying to support herself and launch a career all at the same time, could not have been easy ones either. She was overtired and her health was affected.

A publicity still for *Sabrina* in 1954 shows what Wilder did for Hepburn's image. Suddenly she is glamorous, with sleek hair and a starkly stylish dress by Givenchy – the first time she had worn his clothes.

So she took a year off. The newlyweds honeymooned in an ancient villa 20 miles outside of Rome. Audrey learned to cook, and she also mastered the art of turning a hotel room or rented house into a home for the two of them. (She told one interviewer that she always traveled with at least six trunks, and two of them were filled with personal bric-a-brac, such as silver candlesticks, books and records, favorite photos and paintings.) But even during this restful period, she was thinking about work and looking for the right film to do next.

By the end of 1954, Hepburn was one of the hottest properties in Hollywood. She had once again been nominated for an Academy Award, this time for her performance in *Sabrina*. Although Hepburn lost to Grace Kelly (for *The Country Girl*) her track record – two nominations for her first two movies – was superb. But she took her time to choose her next picture. And her critics leapt on the fact that, when she did, it was a movie that would also star Mel Ferrer.

During the years of her marriage to Ferrer, there were constant rumors about his Svengali-like behavior and its deleterious effect on her career. Some people claimed that he chose all her roles. Others accused him of trying to use her to promote his own career, even if it came at the expense of hers. Hepburn, customarily very reticent about her private life, was unusually vocal in denouncing these reports. She told one reporter angrily, "Why do people keep on saying that Mel makes all my decisions, decides what I am going to play and with whom and where? I, of course, ask his opinion about such things. Any wife would. But Mel is scrupulously correct about not giving an opinion unless it's asked for. This is because we do want to keep our careers separate. But the fact that we value them so much doesn't mean we wouldn't give them up in a minute if our personal happiness was at stake."

That statement is a clue to the real facts. The rumours were obviously exaggerated. Ferrer was often cast as the villain because he tried to protect his wife from the press – and perhaps from the inevitable machinations of the movie business as well. But there is no evidence that he dictated her decisions or tried to manipulate her career for his own advantage.

What *is* clear, and evidenced in the statement Hepburn made to the press, was that marriage had given Audrey Hepburn a slightly different set of priorities. Her career was still important to her, but now she also wanted to arrange things so that she could be with her husband rather than facing the prolonged separations that often accompany show-business marriages. Working together was an obvious solution to the problems of combining marriage and a film career, and it is not surprising that she chose that course when it was at all possible. No doubt that meant turning down some good opportunities; and as she continued to be more successful at the box office than Ferrer, it also no doubt meant that producers who hoped to sign her tried to think of a way to use him. In the long run, the situation was probably more harmful to his career than to hers.

At any rate, Hepburn's next movie was the first of several screen collaborations with Ferrer. It seemed that she was virtually born to

Hepburn was the ideal Natasha in the 1956 production of *War and Peace*; here she is in a scene with Vittorio Gassman.

play the role of Natasha in *War and Peace*. Consider the description of Tolstoy's heroine in the novel: "a dark-eyed girl but full of life, with a wide mouth, her childish bare shoulders, which shrugged and panted in her bodice from her rapid motion, her black hair brushed back, her slender bare arms . . . her shoulders thin, her bosom undefined. And such was Natasha with her wonder, her delight, her shyness."

Everyone agreed that she should play Natasha: the question was, in which movie? In 1954, four different producers announced that they planned to make a film of *War and Peace*. (This odd stampede was probably due in part to the fact that the wide-screen processes had just been developed, and everyone was looking for a property of suitably epic proportions.) The contenders were MGM, David Selznick, Mike Todd, and Dino DeLaurentiis, and each one hinted that Audrey Hepburn would be *his* Natasha. Selznick said his script would be by Ben Hecht and he would start shooting in the summer of 1955. Mike Todd fought back by signing Fred Zinneman to direct and Robert E. Sherwood to write the script. DeLaurentiis got into the race, claimed an associate, because "Mike Todd came to him and tried to get him to put some money into his project. DeLaurentiis said, 'If he hasn't got the money, why don't we do it?'" So he hired King Vidor to direct, and also put him to work on a script. Vidor condensed Tolstoy's one and a half million words into a shooting script in less than a month. Selznick and MGM dropped out of the sweepstakes, but Todd fired out an announcement that he had arranged with Marshal Tito for the cooperation of the Yugoslav army. DeLaurentiis promptly countered with the Italian army, which he claimed was much more photogenic.

Todd finally gave up when Vidor announced that he had actually signed Audrey Hepburn to play Natasha. Vidor had met the Ferrers on holiday in St. Moritz and talked them into the idea. Mel was to be his Prince Andrei (although according to some stories, he had already been signed much earlier).

With two Oscar nominations and one win, plus a Tony to her credit, Hepburn's price for a movie naturally escalated – no more $15,000 appearances for her. At one point, when the contract negotiations were stalled and DeLaurentiis refused to concede some point, her agent, Harry Frings, said, "Fine, make *War and Peace* without her." Needless to say, the producer finally met her demands – a fee of $350,000 with a limit of no more than twelve weeks of work. And Paramount was induced to agree to lend her out by receiving the right to distribute the picture in the US.

Shooting started on July 4, 1955. The Ferrers once again rented the Italian villa in which they had honeymooned; Audrey called it "the most heavenly spot on earth." Famed gossip columnist Louella Parsons visited them during the shooting and raved that their villa "was indeed a garden of beauty, with flowers in full bloom, figs and olives ready for picking. The water for the pool spouted out of an antique carved woman's head. Inside they had added a record-playing machine, some American comforts, but for the most part they had retained the furniture that had belonged for years to their Italian landlord . . ." It took the Ferrers about an hour to drive to the studio in Rome where the film was being shot, but they considered living in the villa worth the commute. Besides, Hepburn's contract stipulated that the studio had to furnish a car and driver.

The shooting of Hepburn's scenes went quickly and smoothly. Vidor said he enjoyed working with her, and he later called her one of the three supremely talented actresses he had directed – the other two were Laurette Taylor and Lillian Gish. He considered her the perfect Natasha, commenting, "While making the film it often occured to me that Audrey, though ideal from my viewpoint, would probably not fulfill a Russian's concept of the part. And yet when the film was made in Russia a few years later, they cast an actress that was exactly Audrey's type. Audrey studied ballet as a child and moves through a scene with a rhythmic grace that is a director's delight."

When Hepburn's scenes were finished, Vidor went on to shoot the rest of the film, and the evidence of the finished product suggests that he was much more comfortable putting actors through their paces on the battlefield than in the drawingroom. He said, "I shot the battle scene myself . . . because I wanted the battles to be clear; I wanted them to mean something. All the *War and Peace* battles were worked out with a stop watch; this group of men go from here to there on a certain count . . . Always a lot of blueprints, a lot of diagrams of what each company, what each fellow must do. Someone on *War and Peace* asked if I ever felt like Napoleon, and I said, 'Hell, Napoleon could only direct one side of a battle; I can direct both sides.'"

But some reports suggest that not all went like clockwork in this production. Arthur Mayer reported with amusement, "Dino has imagin-

Audrey studying the script between takes on *Funny Face.*

ation, unflagging ingenuity, and a capacity for rapid decisive action . . . When his 200 tailors turned out the necessary uniforms but there was a scarcity of buttons, Dino rented an empty factory and manufactured them. On the day 10,000 extras were to appear in front of the camera at one time — probably an all-time record — Dino himself appraised the intelligence quotient of 100 of them and made each responsible for handling 100 of their confreres. When too many accidents occured (in movie battles the object is to avoid casualties) Dino dressed 64 doctors as soldiers and spread them among the combatants to make informed first-aid available in case of need."

But despite all the lavish spectacle — which nearly all reviewers agreed was beautifully photographed — the film did not do as well as its creators had hoped. It did gross over $6 million, but that was only a puny third of the amount taken in by another epic, *The Ten Commandments*. One reason may have been the length of *War and Peace*. The final cut was 208 minutes, considerably longer than most moviegoers were used to sitting still. Another problem was almost certainly the script, which was sometimes awkward and often confusing. A third problem may have been due to the director's limitations. Although the action scenes were all splendid, many people commented that the intimate interior scenes — those between lovers or family members — seemed stilted, airless, unconvincing.

In general, Hepburn received good reviews. William White-bait called her "beautifully, entrancingly alive;" Herbert Luft said her performance was "full of spark, grace, depth, and subtlety." Writing nearly a decade after the release of the film, Simon Brett summed up her appeal: "She dominates an epic picture by refusing to distort her character to the epic mould, rather letting her spontaneity, her very littleness in the face of history, captivate us by its humanity contrasted with the inhumanity of war. She incarnates all that is worth fighting for."

Looking at the film today, Hepburn still seems the perfect physical incarnation of Natasha. She comes across as lovely and vital — perhaps especially in scenes with Ferrer, whose woodenness was singled out by more than one critic. But when she speaks . . . well, the delivery seems affected, frequently without motivation. Part of the problem may well be due to the script, and part to the film's editing (particularly if you happened to see the later version, which has been shortened at the expense of continuity). And Vidor may not have been the right director to bring out the best in her. But even after these excuses, one must admit that Hepburn's chief contribution to the film seems to be personality rather than performance.

However, her next film gave her a chance to dazzle the audience anew. It took prolonged negotiations to put *Funny Face* together. The genesis of the film was a script by Leonard Gershe, which he called *Wedding Day*. He sold it to MGM producer Roger Edens, who decided to beef it up by adding the songs and title of a Broadway musical written in the 1920s by George and Ira Gershwin, called *Funny Face*. He signed former dancer and choreographer Stanley Donen to direct; his impressive credits already included several immortal musicals, such as *On the Town, Singin' in the Rain, Seven Brides for Seven Brothers,* and *It's Always Fair Weather.*

Then Edens approached Fred Astaire and Audrey Hepburn to play the leads, and both seemed amenable. But they were under contract to Paramount, who knew a good thing when they heard it and refused to let them make the film for another studio. In the end, a deal was worked out that sent the MGM property and production team to Paramount. Astaire, who had starred with his sister in the original Gershwin version of *Funny Face*, was quoted as saying he was glad he had waited for things to be worked out on this version. "This could be the last and only opportunity I'd have to work with the great and lovely Audrey and I was not missing it." Hepburn responded to the compliment by hurrying out to Hollywood and spending three months of ten-hour workdays getting in shape to dance with him, under the tutelage of his sister Adele Astaire's former dance coach, Buddy Bradley.

Funny Face was another version of the Cinderella story. Hepburn plays Jo, a shy Greenwich Village intellectual who works as a clerk in a bookstore. One day a fashion photographer (Astaire) drops into her store to use it as a background for a layout he's shooting. When he develops the prints, he realizes that Jo has all the fresh and unusual qualities he is looking for in a model. He and the editor of his magazine (Kay Thompson) badger her until she agrees to become the embodiment of their "new look", and she is

A publicity shot from the Fifties, showing the much-

talked-about "bat-wing brows".

whisked off to Paris to shoot pictures for the forthcoming issue and then launch the look in a live fashion show. Her initial resistance to Astaire eventually turns into a warmer feeling, and after the predictable misunderstandings, they pair up for a happy ending.

Funny Face is very nearly a perfect movie. The script is amusing and witty, with some telling thrusts at both the bohemian life (as it was called in the Fifties) and the world of high fashion. The performances from the two leads are impeccable. Astaire is his usually elegant and relaxed self, and Hepburn has the chance to utilize to the fullest that unique ability to move back and forth from shy girlishness to high-style chic.

As a musical, *Funny Face* has all the hallmarks of Donen's directional freshness and innovation. (It also has the considerable advantage of a lot of terrific Gershwin songs.) Few of the musical numbers seem staged. The title song is introduced most casually, by having Astaire sing it to Hepburn in a darkroom while he is printing up a photo of her face. Hepburn herself sings, "How Long Has This Been Going On?" in a breathy low wistful voice, all alone in the bookstore. The finale takes place outside a small French church, beside a lovely brook, as Astaire and Hepburn drift over the spotless grass in an almost dream-like expression of romance. Hepburn also gets a chance at a solo, a difficult parody of a certain type of intellectual modern dance, that she performs brilliantly in an angular and tortured style that is a comment on its pointlessness.

Any actress who dances with Fred Astaire risks the inevitable comparison with his other partners – many of them better dancers than Hepburn. But she comes off well, and in many ways is reminiscent of his first partner, his sister Adele. Hepburn's long legs and slim body make her a good match for Astaire's own impression of elongation. The completeness and precision of her movements, an obvious reminder of her ballet training, give her an appealing femininity that works well against her partner's masculine jauntiness. Watching them, one is struck by their shared quality of benign remoteness. Neither is emotionally *cold*, but each seems enclosed by some personal bubble of space and air, a visible separateness. Rather than lovers, they seem when they dance to be brother and sister, twin halves of a whole from some classic myth, remarkably similar yet different enough to seem intended as an allegory of the sexes.

The movie is also distinguished by its imaginative use of color and innovative photographic tricks. Both are due to the presence on the set of fashion photographer Richard Avedon as a consultant. Among the most striking visual effects in *Funny Face* for which he was largely responsible: "the dazzling opening with its emphasis on pink as the new color rage in fashion . . . the dance between Audrey and Fred in a photographer's darkroom illuminated solely by the faint glow of a ruby lightbulb . . . the splitscreen views of Paris . . . the soft-focus Corot-influenced scene on the lawn of a rustic French church . . . the way each scene photographed for a magazine layout was frozen as a still picture, first in negative, then as a black-and-white positive, and finally with spots of color added bit by bit to isolated areas." Avedon nonchalantly claimed that everything in the movie

This is the nightclub dance scene from *Funny Face*, in which Hepburn spoofs the angular, intellectual approach to modern dance.

was old hat to still photographers, but it was new and exciting in the movies. Apparently, the demands of protocol created a cumbersome procedure governing Avedon's method of working. "Avedon, hovering just off the edge of the set, conveyed his suggestions to Donen by a system of signals consisting of moving his necktie to various levels of his chest. Donen then conveyed Avedon's idea to Ray June, the cinematographer."

Most of the reviews were good, and Hepburn was generally acclaimed. Edward Jablonski said, "Audrey Hepburn, making her musical debut in this filmusical, sings winningly, though with no great voice, and dances very well." *Newsweek* praised, "The charm, the elegance, the nutty pictorial poetry to be found in the classier fashion photographs have all been preserved on the screen." Simon Brett perceptively commented, "So long after giving up ballet as a career, she is an actress dancing rather than a dancer acting, like Astaire, but she gives well of both, just as while singing she is constantly acting." One dissenting voice came from *The Harvard Lampoon*, which named *Funny Face* as one of the Ten Worst Pictures of 1957, and made an additional snide citation for "Most Appalling Example of the Inadequacy of Our Present Social Security Program: Fred Astaire, forced once more out of retirement to don his high-heeled tap shoes and pursue Audrey Hepburn before an ill-focused camera lens in *Funny Face*." The box office was good in all the major cities, but apparently the film was too sophisticated for small-town audiences, and it was the first of Hepburn's films to fail to become one of the top moneymakers of the year of its release. Today it is considered a classic, and is frequently shown in revival houses and also on television.

When the filming of *Funny Face* was completed, Hepburn stayed on in Paris to begin her next project. Ferrer was working there on *Paris Does Strange Things* and later in the south of France on *The Vintage*, so an extended stay in Paris was personally convenient. Besides, it was a film she had wanted to do for some time – in fact, she had announced two years earlier that she would appear in it. Then it was delayed, and *Funny Face* came up.

The film was *Love in the Afternoon*, directed by Billy Wilder, with whom she had greatly enjoyed working. The movie was based on the novel *Ariane* by Claude Anet, and it had already been dramatized twice previously, once as a silent film and once in French. Its appeal seems to lie in the fact that it is yet another fairytale story.

Hepburn of course has the Cinderella role and once again wins the handsome prince. She plays Ariane, the young and lovely daughter of a somewhat cynical private detective (Maurice Chevalier) who specializes in acquiring evidence of adultery. He is hired to entrap the wife of a client with her playboy lover, American millionaire Frank Flannagan (Gary Cooper). Ariane overhears the husband plotting to kill Frank and in true do-gooder spirit, she hurries to his hotel to warn him of his danger. She saves him by taking the adulterous wife's place when the outraged husband bursts into the room – and of course, it isn't long before the playboy tries to make the substitution a reality instead of a fiction. Ariane naturally falls in love, and she pretends to be a worldly sophisticate in order to win her man, whose tastes are presumably . . . exotic. But her virginal innocence eventually shines through and saves her from Frank's amorous attacks (the fact that her father threatens him doesn't hurt either.) When he realizes that her worldliness is only a ploy, it appears that the mismatched pair must part. But at the very last moment, as Cooper is going away on a train, he scoops her up in his arms, makes an honorable proposal, and all is well.

The similarities of this plot to that of Hepburn's first successful vehicle, *Gigi*, are obvious. The innocent girl, whose intentions run along purely moral and traditional lines; her cynical family, with their knowledge of the ways of the world; the older, more experienced hero, whom the girl meets through her family; the clash of two sets of values; the triumph of innocence and conventionality. These are not simple Cinderella stories though; they also have an element of Beauty and the Beast. Entranced by the love of a beautiful and pure young woman, the wicked hero gives up his vices and regains his own goodness. Hepburn's physical presence is a powerful asset in convincing us that such an improbable transformation could take place.

This overtone of the Beast makes the role of the playboy in *Love in the Afternoon* a difficult one to play, and many people felt that Gary Cooper was badly miscast in the film (one of the last of his career). Wilder's original intention had been to use Cary Grant, but he was busy elsewhere; he's the one star Wilder has never been able to make a film with. So Cooper was signed instead. He apparently had misgivings about accepting the role. He worried that playing the part of the caddish playboy might tarnish his all-American hero image. He was afraid he would appear unconvincing and awkward. He was especially concerned about a scene in which he had to dance with Hepburn and grumbled that he had two left feet (and Wilder, who tried to teach him the steps, agreed).

Most of all, Cooper feared that he simply looked too old to be Audrey Hepburn's lover. Wilder later agreed that "Coop was too old for Audrey," and the critics certainly harped on it (of course, they had made the same complaint about Humphrey Bogart and Fred Astaire). The story *is* supposed to be about the romance between a worldly roué and a young girl, but the disparity in the two principals' apparent ages made the love scenes teeter perilously on the edge of bad taste. Wilder was unusually tactful in shooting Cooper and Hepburn together; as one critic remarked, "The camera takes Cooper in silhouette, or in a mirror, or the back of his head, and once, his feet." Physical passion between the pair was merely suggested by the removal of a glove, the slither of a fur coat dropped to the floor. This discreet limitation of actual contact between the lovers leaves a curious coldness at the center of a supposedly romantic picture.

The film is much more satisfactory when it deals with the relationship between father and daughter. Indeed, it may be the very success of this portrayal that makes the audience uncomfortable about Ariane's relationship with a lover who looks at least as old as her father. B.F. Dick comments, "Early in the film, Wilder uses a long shot to depict the kind of life the widower and his daughter have together. As Chevasse [Maurice Chevalier] enters their flat, Ariane is practicing the cello; Wilder frames both of them in the same shot. There is no fluttery rush to the door, no outstretched arms, no squealed greetings. Father and daughter know each other's habits." There is between this father and daughter a warmth, a degree of understanding, that makes it easy to see why Wilder's own daughter cites *Love in the Afternoon* as one of her favourite films.

Although the box office business was good, it was not sensational. Nor were the critics whole-hearted in their praise. Courtland Phipps called it "amusing, bright, and incredible," although he went on to complain that Hepburn's "decidedly outré appeal is getting less and less, and has worn so thin it barely covers the exigencies of this very ably directed entertainment." *Newsweek* was more complimentary, calling the movie a "tripping, buoyant and unusually engaging comedy, a light love lyric, perfectly balanced and full of style." Many critics pointed out the similarity to the films of Lubitsch (with whom Wilder had worked as a writer) but declared *Love in the Afternoon* to be second-rate Lubitsch. There was a widespread feeling that only Hepburn's charm and sweetness held the improbable fiction together.

Hepburn's next venture was an unexpected change. She and Ferrer starred as the ill-fated lovers, Crown Prince Rudolph of Austria and his mistress Maria Vetsera, in a made-for-television spectacular called *Mayerling*. Most of the reviews harped on the statistics (always a bad sign): a budget of $500,000; a cast of 200; more than 20 different sets; lavish costumes trimmed with gold braid and real gold buttons. *Mayerling* was produced and directed by Anatole Litvak, who had made a movie version twenty years earlier, starring Charles Boyer and Danielle Darrieux, that was a real tear-jerker. Unfortunately, somewhere along the way he lost the emotional impact of the story in this version. There was too much spectacle and too little emotion; the lavishness of the budget seems to have swamped the human aspects of the lovers' drama. There was a certain amount of praise for the high-mindedness of the attempt, but most viewers probably agreed with critic John Crosby, who said, "The lovers seem more fated to bore each other to death than to end their illicit alliance in a murder-suicide pact."

At this point in Hepburn's career, fans and critics alike agreed that her five movie roles had largely been variations on a single theme. She was always the fairytale princess, the youthful virginal figure who could lose her heart but never her innocence; as one writer put it, "a moon goddess whose virginity is never really lost because it is always restored." She was sometimes funny, sometimes touching, but her emotions were always *girlish*.The audience smiled at her but never felt with her.

To stake her claim to consideration as a truly accomplished actress, she needed a part that extended her range and called for deeper, more mature emotions. She found it in *The Nun's Story*. It was a Warner Brothers film, directed by Fred Zinneman. The sensitive script, written by Robert Anderson, was based on a book by Kathryn C. Hulme, which sold over three million copies in the US and was translated into twelve languages. Hulme's book told the real-life story of a woman she had met in 1945 (she gave her the fictionalized name of Gabrielle van der Mal) when they were both working for a UN relief mission in Germany. Van der Mal had only several months earlier left the Belgian convent in which she had taken her vows as a nun.

Hepburn and co-star Fred Astaire take a break during the filming of *Funny Face.*

E·50·6 POR·8

The Nun's Story depicts the spiritual progress of Sister Luke. The movie opens when the Belgian doctor's daughter (Hepburn) enters a convent. Through a series of vignettes, we follow her through her novitiate and her struggle to internalize her vows of obedience and humility. Her difficulty is emphasized by the sympathetic head of the Order (Dame Edith Evans) who tells her that the life of a nun "is in many ways a life against nature." After she takes her final vows, she is sent to a hospital in the Belgian Congo, where she encounters an agnostic doctor (Peter Finch) who warns her that she remains too individualistic for the demands of her vocation. She overworks herself into a state of exhaustion and then contracts tuberculosis, although she is eventually cured. She returns to Belgium just as World War II breaks out and is sent to a hospital that treats the casualties of both sides in the fighting. When she learns that her father (Dean Jagger) has been gunned down by the Nazis while tending wounded refugees, she is overwhelmed by a feeling of hatred for the killers. Recognizing that she has not yet attained a state of true spiritual grace, she leaves the Order, to embark on resistance activities.

Hepburn knew the role of the nun was a wonderful chance to prove herself as an actress. She told one interviewer, "If I had been offered The Nun's Story three years ago, I wouldn't have done it. Now I am slightly better equipped and my range is a little wider." She accepted the role despite the fact that it would entail her first long separation from her husband, who was working on a film in Hollywood, while she was doing studio work in Rome. Another drawback was that she would have to travel to Africa, where work on location imposed rugged physical demands. Dozens of inoculations were required before she could even leave. Once she got there, she faced the usual problems of heat exhaustion, poisonous snakes, and long grueling days. In addition, there was the rather frightening work on location at an actual leper colony and the painful bites of a Magistra monkey that was supposed to be Sister Luke's pet.

Much of The Nun's Story's success (it was nominated for eight Academy Awards) was due to a painstaking attention to detail. All locations were as authentic as possible, not only in Africa but also in Brussels, Bruges, and Antwerp. Hepburn apparently spent some time in convents talking to nuns, so that she might better understand the life she was portraying. Director Zinneman insisted that she should also meet the real-life Sister Luke, then a nurse in Los Angeles. The woman later recalled that Hepburn "didn't really want to meet me. She felt the story was too much of my private life. She just sat there and looked at me and didn't ask any questions."

The sets were carefully designed for authenticity, and the rituals of convent life were beautifully choreographed (seventy members of Rome's Royal Opera ballet were recruited to play the nuns in these scenes.) The photography by cameraman Fritz Planer is an integral part of the film's significance, especially in its contrast of the cool black-and-white world of the nuns with the hot exotic color of the Congo. According to one report, Zinneman's passion for verisimilitude was carried to the point that "two weeks before his actresses appeared before the camera, each of them was denied the use of makeup and forbidden exposure to the sun. Makeup man Alberto di Rossi's job was to effect a non-makeup and make certain there were no traces of artificial red showing on the lips of the women portraying nuns."

The results of all this care were impressive. The woman whose story was the basis of the movie saw it four times and commented that she was afraid to see it again, "because if I do I'm going to run right back to the convent. When you see the chapel, all those nuns . . . I could just sit there and cry my eyes out, not with regret or anything but because of the beauty of it." Although Zinneman admitted that, "Some people, mostly on the outside, mostly non-Catholics, say that our view of religion is superficial," he went on to stress, "People who are actually in the orders to a very large extent feel that we have done a good job." As apparently did the Motion Picture Academy. *The Nun's Story* was nominated for Best Picture and Zinneman for Best Director. Hepburn was among the nominees for Best Actress, her third nomination in six pictures. The screenplay and photography were also cited.

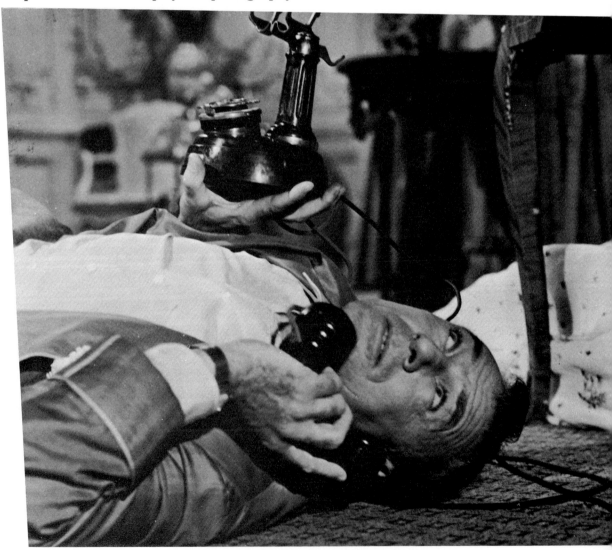

Audiences were equally enthusiastic. The picture grossed more than $6 million, which made it the fifth most financially successful movie of 1959. And critics were most flattering, both about the movie in general and Hepburn's performance in particular. Henry Hart, writing in *Films in Review*, said, "The nun is played by Audrey Hepburn with such complete understanding of the full content of each scene that her performance will forever silence those who have thought her less an actress than a symbol of the sophisticated child/woman (exclusively a contemporary idea). In *The Nun's Story*, Miss Hepburn reveals the kind of acting talent that can project inner feelings of both depth and complexity so skillfully you must scrutinize her intently on a second and third viewing of the film to perceive how she does it. Her portrayal of Sister Luke is one of the great performances of the screen." *Variety* called it her finest performance, and Campbell Dixon announced, "As the nun Audrey Hepburn achieves a new stature; if this beautiful and touching performance doesn't earn her all the Oscars that are

In *Love in the Afternoon*, Billy Wilder softened Hepburn's style, with a demure hairdo and "sweet" clothes. Here she romps with leading man Gary Cooper.

going, juries are going to look even sillier than usual." So much for the people who voted to give the Oscar to Simone Signoret. But Hepburn did win the New York Film Critics Award, as well as the British Film Industry's annual Best Actress award.

As soon as *The Nun's Story* was finished, Hepburn went right to work on her next project. It was to be another film with her husband; this time he would direct her. She looked forward to it happily, saying, "Oh, it's going to be so much fun to be with Mel and to be excited about the same things and not to go off to different parts of the world." She told a reporter that she was not worried about the problems of having a husband for a director. "Mel won't have any trouble with me. I don't think I'm unreasonably difficult. I like being directed. I don't know what to do myself. Of course, there are certain things on the set that I have an instinct about. What I do worry about is that I might hesitate to suggest something because I wouldn't want him to think that I'm interfering. Of course, any contribution of mine would be minimal, but sometimes one does think of something, you know." It all sounds very like the contortions of a woman trying to place herself at a level beneath that of a man she secretly fears is her inferior.

She concluded the interview by saying firmly, "This is his great chance [to direct]. He has studied so hard for it. All his life he loved this particular story." The story was *Green Mansions*, the haunting novel by W.H. Hudson. It is a lyrical tale that celebrates the spirit of nature and the loneliness of the human soul. Its unforgettable heroine is Rima, a lovely girl who is the last descendant of a tribe of nature-worshipping people whose language was a sweet warble like that of the birds.

Rights to the novel were purchased by RKO in 1931; the studio wanted King Vidor to direct and Dolores Del Rio to play Rima. But the idea was abandoned due to the difficulty of obtaining a satisfactory script. After a few more abortive attempts, RKO let the rights go. They were purchased by MGM in 1946 with the intention of creating a sort of musical version starring Yma Sumac, the extraordinary Peruvian singer with long black hair, the features of an Inca, and a vocal range of four octaves. That exotic idea also came to naught. Then Alan Lerner was going to write a script as a vehicle for Elizabeth Taylor, but that fell through (a blessing to audiences everywhere). Producer Pandro Berman actually filmed a few scenes with fragile Italian actress Pier Angeli, but that version ground to a halt when the star became pregnant.

Then writer Dorothy Kingsley became interested in the project. Her previous writing credits included radio scripts for Bob Hope and Edgar Bergen, and she also did the screenplay for *Pal Joey*. She was a less-than-ideal writer to tackle Hudson's mystical allusive novel, but she was enthusiastic and actually produced a script, more than you can say about anyone else involved with it so far She took her script to MGM producer Edmund Grainger and talked him into doing the movie. As part of the earlier deal through which MGM had sent its *Funny Face* team to Paramount, they were owed in return a picture starring Hepburn – and Ferrer as director was part of the package. Thinking that Hepburn would make an ideal Rima, Grainger approached Ferrer, and the deal was quickly made.

The Nun's Story, for which she received another

Oscar nomination is considered by many to be

Audrey Hepburn's best performance.

The plot of *Green Mansions* is somewhat nebulous. A young man, Abel (Anthony Perkins), who has made powerful political enemies, flees for his life and hides out in the jungle with a tribe of South American Indians. He notices that they are afraid to enter a nearby forest, which they claim is haunted. He determines to explore it and follows strange bird sounds until he catches a glimpse of a beautiful but elusive girl (Hepburn). She saves his life when he is bitten by a snake and takes him to the hut where she lives with Nuflo (Lee J. Cobb) an old man who has protected her from the Indians; they consider her a dangerous spirit and want to kill her. At Rima's insistence, the trio makes a journey to try to find the "place where she belongs" but the quest proves fruitless and it is at last clear to Rima that she is the only person of her race left in the world. Abel comforts her and offers to live with her in the forest forever. She returns to make a home for him. Traveling at a slower pace, he arrives some days later. He finds the hut in which she and Nuflo lived gone, and then he learns to his sorrow that the Indians managed to trap her in a tree and set it afire. He takes revenge on those who killed her and then faces the lonely mourning for the rest of his life.

Ferrer obviously attempted to turn the movie into more than just another Sheena Queen of the Jungle flick. He hired Hector Villa-Lobos to write special music, and Katherine Dunham to stage a native dance. He used good character actors, including Nehemiah Persoff, Henry Silva, and Sessue Hayakawa. He added special effects. He dressed his lovely star in a glittering gold dress and photographed her moving half-unseen through the forest in some beautiful sequences. He went on location, in Venezuela and Guyana, to shoot much of the film, and the soft-focus photography of cameraman Joseph Rothenburg is one of the film's most successful aspects.

But there is much that is wrong with *Green Mansions*. One major problem is the script: as one critic put it, "No script could have destroyed more of Hudson's magic." Another problem lies in the choice of Anthony Perkins as Abel. He was simply not convincing – seems too high strung and neurotic himself to make a good foil to Rima – and in some scenes his acting borders on the grotesque. A more complex problem is the difficulty in using *Green Mansions* as a vehicle for a star. Rima is an elusive, other-worldly being; Hudson, in fact, never even gives a physical description of his bird-girl. But stars are in films because cameras (and audiences) love their faces. Alas, every time we see Hepburn looming up on the screen, Rima loses a little more of her essential mystery. (Those primitive peoples who believe that the camera steals the soul are not entirely wrong.) It doesn't matter whether Hepburn plays the role well or badly; it's her palpable physical presence that undermines the heart of the film.

If a star had to be cast in *Green Mansions*, then Hepburn was surely the best choice. Critic Adelaide Comerford remarked, "Miss Hepburn's asexual form, big brown eyes, and lovely voice are suited to the child-of-nature concept we all carry with us and Hudson apotheosized. She was often believable in this difficult role and at least once, genuinely moving (when she spoke of her need to find out what she was and what she was seeking)."

In general, audiences were disenchanted and the critics harsh. Several referred to it as a debacle, and most of them blamed it on Ferrer. One wrote savagely, "If Miss Hepburn won't change husbands, or directors, she at least owes it to her public to change her brand of toothpaste. Because in Ferrer's fiasco, she looks as if she had been given an overdose of chlorophyll. In fact, the whole thing, even the authentic background footage, has an appalling greenish patina that makes it look as if it had been filmed in a decaying parsley patch." Even the critics who refrained from decrying Hepburn's green teeth had almost nothing positive to say.

Luckily, Hepburn had little time to regret the failure of *Green Mansions*. It was released at nearly the same time as *The Nun's Story*, so she was able to ignore the condemnation of one film and enjoy the praise of the other. And events in her personal life also gave her something to be joyful about. Only a few months after learning she had lost the Oscar to Simone Signoret (for *Room at the Top*) Hepburn gave birth to her first child, Sean Ferrer. She was quoted as saying, "Success isn't too important for a woman. And with the baby, I felt I had everything a wife could wish for."

In the 1959 release, *Green Mansions*, Audrey Hepburn was directed by her husband as she played Rima, the elusive girl of the forest.

the Sixties

The first Hepburn film released in the decade of the Sixties was *The Unforgiven*, although it was actually shot in late 1959. Her role was another significant departure from the fairytale princesses that had largely been the core of the Hepburn screen persona in the Fifties. Whether or not it was a successful innovation is another question.

The Unforgiven was originally a novel by Alan LeMay. The screenplay adaptation was written by Ben Maddow (who was responsible for *The Asphalt Jungle* and other outstanding scripts) under the auspices of the independent production company formed by Ben Hecht and Burt Lancaster. Hecht-Hill-Lancaster went after the stars first. Burt wanted to play the hero, which by no coincidence was a perfect role for him. They then managed to sign up a wonderful supporting cast that included Charles Bickford, Lillian Gish, and Audie Murphy. Hepburn agreed to play the heroine, a step that surely indicated a desire to extend herself beyond typecasting.

With this wonderful package assembled, Hecht-Hill-Lancaster went to John Huston and asked him to direct. Agreeably impressed by the strength of the cast and the talent of the scriptwriter, Huston agreed, even though he did not endorse the vision of the movie that was advanced by the producers. He commented later in his autobiography, "I thought I saw in Maddow's script the potential for a more serious – and better – film than either he or Hecht-Hill-Lancaster had originally contemplated; I wanted to turn it into the story of racial intolerance in a frontier town, a comment on the real nature of community 'morality,' What they wanted was what I had unfortunately signed on to make when I accepted the job in the first place – a swashbuckler about a larger-than-life frontiersman. This difference of intention did not become an issue until we were very close to shooting time, and quite mistakenly I agreed to stick it out, thus violating my own conviction that a picture-maker should undertake nothing but what he believes in – regardless. From that moment, the entire picture turned sour."

Unfortunately, the film that made it to the screen shows many signs of this underlying conflict of intentions. It is the story of a family

In *Breakfast at Tiffany's*, Hepburn was once again dressed by Givenchy, and this simple black sheath dress was one of the most popular of his designs.

achieving tenuous prosperity as ranchers under the driving impetus of Ben (Burt Lancaster) the head of the family. He protects his mother (Lillian Gish) and his sister (Hepburn) and bullies his younger brothers (Audie Murphy and Doug McClure) into productivity. After a certain number of standard home-on-the-range scenes – the men returning from the cattle drive, mom playing the pyanner, the women's work of churning butter, sis galloping furiously to nowhere on a spirited buckskin – events take on a darker tone with the arrival of a sword-waving lunatic who denounces Hepburn as an Indian. In no time at all the plot thickens. The Kiowas are stirred up and want to get Hepburn back, they kill her fiancé, and his family turns against her and *her* family when her mother finally confesses – to Ben's astonishment – that the accusation is true. Audie Murphy deserts and the rest of the family prepares to defend themselves against an onslaught by the determined Kiowas, led by the girl's brother (John Saxon, made up to emphasize his cheekbones). The whole issue of racism in frontier communities is then dropped permanently in favor of the usual settlers-against-the-Indians thrills, and the picture ends with Gish dead, Murphy back in the family, and Hepburn and Lancaster engaged and apparently planning to live happily ever after – no mention of what the neighbors are going to say.

In *The Unforgiven*, Audrey Hepburn dressed in homespun and impersonated a girl of the prairie.

The picture was shot in Durango, Mexico, and life on location seemed unusually hazardous. Audie Murphy nearly drowned in a lake (an old war-wound in his hip made him unable to swim) and Hepburn was thrown from her horse and suffered a fractured vertebra. That delayed the shooting for three months, while Hepburn was nursed back to health by guess who . . . the real-life Sister Luke! Ah, Hollywood.

It seems doubtful whether all the trouble was worth it. *The Unforgiven* was a modest box office draw, and the reviews were definitely mixed. One of the harshest came from Huston himself, who recently labelled *The Unforgiven* the only one of his pictures he actually dislikes: "Despite some good performances, the overall tone is bombastic and over-inflated. Everybody in it is bigger than life." Critic Dwight MacDonald was among those who considered Hepburn badly miscast as the Indian girl turned settler. "Miss Hepburn essays the tomboy-cum-child-of-nature, but when she tries to be vital, she becomes even more lifeless than usual. She is not an actress, she is a model, with her stiff meager body and her blank face full of good bone structure. She has the model's narcissism, not the actress' introversion. The door is giving way, the roof is burning, her ma has expired from an Injun bullet, she has been given the pistol with one shot in it for herself ('Is it pain to die, Ben?') Lancaster is peering grimly through the smoke waiting for the final charge, and here is Audrey, somehow immaculate despite her carefully smudged face, showing us her Fine Bone Structure." Even Hepburn fans are likely to find her prairie accent rather jolting, and the film is too confused to allow her (or any other actor involved) much of a chance to develop a character.

Critic Simon Brett calls *The Unforgiven* a turning point in Hepburn's screen persona because it is her first genuine departure from innocence. In the penultimate climax of the final reel she shoots and kills her Indian brother as he comes in the door to take her back home. However desperate the circumstances that led to the event, there is no escaping the fact that she has killed — in fact, that she has committed the crime of fratricide (remember, as Oedipus found out, the gods don't care whether you recognize these relatives or not). This presages a change in her screen image during the Sixties. She can still be child-like, but she no longer projects that image of intense, other-worldly purity. Now she is more likely to indulge in those compromises we all come to sooner or later. Her very next film, *Breakfast at Tiffany's*, gives definition to this new image.

The movie was based on a novella by Truman Capote, published to popular success and critical acclaim in 1958. The story describes the adventures of heroine Holly Golightly. A contemporary book review in *Time* claimed, "She's the hottest kitten ever to hit the typewriter keys of Truman Capote. She's a cross between a grown-up Lolita and a teen-age Auntie Mame. A piquantly wacky ex-hillbilly who lives in a Manhattan upper East Side brownstone, she is a kind of expense account tramp . . . alone and a little afraid in a lot of beds she never made."

Rights to the novel were purchased by Jurow-Shepherd, an independent production company. They hired George Axelrod to write a screenplay, and he had the difficult task of trying to translate Capote's story

PARAMOUNT PRESENTS

AUDREY HEPBURN

GEORGE PEPPARD IN

BREAKFAST AT TIFFANY'S

A JUROW-SHEPHERD PRODUCTION

Directed by
BLAKE EDWARDS
Produced by
MARTIN JUROW and
RICHARD SHEPHERD
Screenplay by
GEORGE AXELROD
sed on the Novel by TRUMAN CAPOTE
—HENRY MANCINI

CO-STARRING

PATRICIA BUDDY MARTIN
NEAL · EBSEN · BALSA
AND
MICKEY ROONE

TECHNICOLOR®
A PARAMOUNT RELEASE

Hepburn speaks to Alec Guinness in a scene near the
end of *Lavender Hill Mob*.

A swinging Sixties look

◁ This is the "before" version of Hepburn in *Funny Face*; it makes one wonder why the fashion editors thought she needed making over.

▷ In *Bloodline*, Hepburn was once again costumed by Givenchy, in a somewhat more vulnerable rendition of her customary elegance.

▽ Fred Astaire captures Audrey's slim Givenchy line in *Funny Face*.

Hepburn with Bogart in *Sabrina Fair*

Picture Show & FILM PICTORIAL

THE PAPER FOR PEOPLE WHO GO TO THE PICTURES

October 3rd, 1953 Vol. 61 No. 1592 Every Tuesday 3D

Picture Show

THE PAPER FOR PEOPLE WHO GO TO THE PICTURES

Vol. 63 October 23rd, 1954 No. 1647 Every Tuesday

& FILM PICTORIAL

AUDREY HEPBURN & GREGORY PECK IN "Roman Holiday"

AUDREY HEPBURN & WILLIAM HOLDEN "Sabrina Fair"

Audrey as Natasha in *War and Peace*

By the end of the decade of the Fifties, Audrey Hepburn was beginning to tone down her high-contrast *maquillage* in favor of a more elegant look.

Hepburn's classic Fifties look

Little Audrey . . . Sexy At Last. From a scene *Two For The Road* with Albert Finney.

Audrey with first husband, Mel Ferrer

△ Another shot from *Young Wives Tale* shows Hepburn in an uncharacteristically baggy garment.

▷ This outfit from *Charade* embodies Audrey Hepburn's personal style: "I prefer very plain clothes, very uncluttered. I don't like distracting details. I like very simple gloves, shoes, and hats. Nothing should take away from the basic line of the clothes."

◁ Sixties hairdo and black-rimmed eyes are the hallmarks of Audrey's look in *How To Steal A Million*.

△ In order to pull off a successful robbery in *How To Steal A Million*, Hepburn must dress up as a charlady, in an outfit faintly reminiscent of the Eliza Doolittle costume.

Hepburn sporting a distinctive Givenchy outfit

A moment of suspense in *Wait Until Dark*

Hepburn's bouffant hairdo

Audrey at the time of *Robin and Marian*

of call girls, drug dealers, and kept men into something acceptable to the moral standards of the American mass audience in 1960. Blake Edwards agreed to direct; his credits at that time included *Operation Petticoat* and *High Times*.

Obviously, the casting of Holly Golightly was the most crucial decision for the movie's success. Marilyn Monroe was apparently the first choice, and at the time it was rumored she was about to be signed, there were a number of stories in the press about how Capote had modelled his heroine on Monroe. That claim is hard to believe if you've ever read the novella. Consider Capote's description of Holly. One character says, "I see pieces of her all the time, a flat little bottom, any skinny girl that walks fast and straight —" A few pages later, Capote describes her in more detail: "For all her chic thinness, she had an almost breakfast-cereal air of health, a soap and lemon cleanness, a rough pink darkening in the cheeks. Her mouth was large, her nose upturned. A pair of dark glasses blotted out her eyes. It was a face beyond childhood, yet this side of belonging to a woman." Does that sound anything like Marilyn Monroe? (*Of course not*, you answer.) Who does it sound like? Audrey Hepburn, of course.

As soon as Monroe turned it down, Hepburn was offered the part. She commented, "I didn't think I was right for it. I had believed all the publicity that claimed Truman Capote had written it for Marilyn Monroe, and I hesitated to read the script. But once I did, I found it irresistible." Interestingly, as soon as she was signed, a quote from Truman Capote suddenly surfaced, claiming *Breakfast at Tiffany's* was actually "a mawkish Valentine to Audrey Hepburn." Hepburn went to work on the film in mid-September, 1960, when her new baby was only about ten weeks old.

The plot of *Breakfast at Tiffany's* centers entirely on the adventures of Holly Golightly, a young girl recently moved to New York from Tulip, Texas. She supports herself on the money her dates give her for "the powder room attendant," which is the movie's tactful way of explaining that she is a call girl. She also earns a stipend by visiting an elderly gangster in Sing Sing each week, bringing back messages that she doesn't realize are instructions for the members of his dope ring. She meets Paul, an impoverished writer (George Peppard) who is more or less a gigolo, kept by a wealthy society lady (Patricia Neal). At first Paul is nothing more to Holly than an ally to fight off her desparate fear that happiness may never come. As part of her attempt to find it, she eventually becomes engaged to a sort of comic-book rich Latin lover (Jose-Luis de Vilallonga) but is obviously beginning to fall in love with Paul. Her elderly ex-husband (Buddy Ebsen) turns up and tells Paul more about Holly's insecure past and her almost incestuous attachment to her brother Fred. When she learns that Fred is dead, she turns angry and bitter and rejects both friends and lovers — and even her cat. In a bittersweet ending, she frantically searches the alleyway, in the rain, for the lost cat, through which we are meant to conclude that she is learning to take responsibility for her actions at last, and that she and Paul might just succeed in making it together without further help from wealthy "patrons."

Holly Golightly and Cat struggle to wake up in *Breakfast at Tiffany's*.

Viewed strictly as a story, the movie version is frequently confusing, especially when it is trying to tidy up Capote's often rather sordid facts of life. For example, Patricia Neal's character seems to be keeping Paul, one can only presume as a lover, but at the same time it is implied that she is a lesbian. Then there is the inscrutable presence of Mickey Rooney as the Japanese Mr. Yunioshi; his value to the plot — or the picture — is certainly debatable.

But really this somewhat convoluted plot is not important. *Breakfast at Tiffany's* succeeds primarily as a mood piece; when we view it today, it seems appropriately symbolic of the Sixties. Some of the images have great staying power. Examples are the opening shot, with Holly emerging from a cab in an evening dress and dark glasses, to lean her head against the cool glass of Tiffany's window and breakfast on the black coffee and donut she had brought along with her; Holly in an outrageously campy dress that is a sort of spoof of the high-fashion look, with strangely frosted hair and a three-foot cigarette holder; Paul and Doc walking through the fallen leaves in Central Park and talking about Holly's past; Holly pensively playing "Moon River" (the song won an Oscar for Henry Mancini and Johnny Mercer) on her guitar by the fire escape; and Holly in the pouring rain looking for that runaway cat.

Even in its toned-down screen version, *Breakfast at Tiffany's* was a bit too far ahead of public attitudes to be one of the top money-making films of 1961, but it did good business in the cities, and it was by and large a critical success. Hepburn was nominated by the Academy for Best Actress (her fourth time in eight pictures: she was still batting .500) and George Axelrod was nominated for Best Script. Although neither won – that was the year Sophia Loren took the Oscar for *Two Women* – it was a good showing for a light comedy.

Hepburn's own reviews were quite good. Ellen Fitzpatrick's is characteristic: "She is certainly lovelier than ever. Her recent pregnancy has put some much-needed flesh on her bones and softened the once-gaunt outlines of her face. And Franz Planer's color photography of her is art that will elicit a response from even non-Hepburnians. Furthermore, Miss Hepburn's acting ability is also better than ever, so I suppose it's no wonder everyone connected with this picture gave above and beyond the call of duty." One dissenting voice came from scenarist Axelrod, who criticized Hepburn for her unwillingness to do anything that would make the character she played unsympathetic. Certainly that refusal made Holly a simpler character in the movie than she was in the novella – but it probably also made her a better heroine of an amusing and romantic film.

The true heroine of *Breakfast at Tiffany's* was an amalgam of Audrey Hepburn and Capote's Holly Golightly, as Hepburn the actress was wise enough to recognize. And just as she brought something of her own myth to the role, she took away from it some aspects of Holly to alter the future Hepburn persona. She was now more sophisticated, less trusting – and oddly, although Holly was meant to be only 19, also less girlish.

Hepburn's next screen role was not such a happy fit between the Hepburn persona and the filmic character. The picture in question was *The Children's Hour*. It was based on the play of the same name written in 1934 by Lillian Hellman, her first success, and it was about the damage done by a lying child's assertion that two of her school-teachers are involved in a lesbian relationship. Samuel Goldwyn bought the film rights at the time of the play's run on Broadway, for $35,000, and MGM turned it into a picture called *These Three*, with a script adapted by Hellman to get past the Hollywood censor (the accusation was changed to one of adultery, apparently a more acceptable sin.) *These Three* was directed by William Wyler and starred Miriam Hopkins and Merle Oberon as the schoolteachers. Wyler felt he had made as good a film as the standards of 1936 would allow, but he wanted a chance to make a movie that was closer to Hellman's original drama. He persuaded the Mirisch brothers to buy the rights from MGM (by 1959, the price had increased tenfold, to $350,000) and asked Hellman to start work on a new script. She began a treatment but dropped out of the project at the time of Dashiell Hammett's final illness and death. So the writing job was turned over to John Michael Hayes, a veteran of some of Hitchcock's best films. Shooting was scheduled to begin in the fall of 1960, as soon as Hepburn had finished her work on *Breakfast at Tiffany's*.

Hepburn was delighted to be working once again with Wyler. In an interview given at the time, she recalled working with him on

In *The Children's Hour* (1962) Hepburn co-starred

with Shirley MacLaine.

her first film: "Willie . . . liberated me. He gave me confidence where before there was only a sort of numbed fear. He taught me what it was all about, showed me the way, and turned me loose. We are in such close communication we hardly have to talk. I *know* when he feels it's wrong."

In *The Children's Hour*, Hepburn plays the part of Karen Wright, who opens a girl's school with her friend Martha Dobie (Shirley MacLaine) and looks forward to eventual marriage to her fiancé (James Garner). Then a sulky student (twelve-year-old Karen Balkin) convinces another girl she has seen Martha make "unnatural" advances to Karen, and the malicious gossip quickly spreads. Although the accusation is untrue, Martha is soon demoralized into confessing "tendencies" toward such feelings, and in an excess of shame over the lying gossip and the privately-acknowledged truth, she hangs herself. The picture ends with Karen's fiancé, who had deserted when the gossip first began, walking her away from the cemetery, into the Hollywood sunset that suggests the eventual dawn of happiness.

One obvious problem with *The Children's Hour* was the script, which can't make up its mind just how faithful to the spirit of Hellman's original it really wants to be. Wyler was quoted at the time he began the picture as saying, "When we made the picture the last time, what we put out was a watered version. We couldn't put it on the way we wanted to because the public wasn't ready for that sort of thing yet. Now, they are." But the end product indicates that perhaps he wasn't as sure of that as he sounded. The Mirisch brothers put pressure on the writer to deliver a script that would be able to earn Production Code approval. And the play's bleakness seemed troubling for a movie audience: several different endings were tried for the screen version, and the final version is an obvious compromise, an attempt to create a whiff of last-minute happiness for at least a few of the characters without undercutting the stern message conveyed by Martha's death. Wyler himself may have undermined the seriousness of his intention by casting as his tragic heroines two actresses best known to the public for their light comic touch.

Although it is not easy to find the film being shown today, it repays watching for the strength of the two lead performances. Shirley MacLaine is no less than outstanding in several of her scenes — several visibly surprised critics labelled it the best acting of her career — and Hepburn is less mannered than in most previous roles, showing a willingness to submerge herself to the demands of the character.

But much of the script is unconvincing, and the theme is treated with an unattractive mixture of embarrassment and censure. It's not surprising that the reviews were harsh. Brendan Gill commented, "From the way Mr. Wyler carries on, you might suppose that he had only just learned about the existence of such relationships and was feeling distinctly let down by human nature. Grown men and women whisper fearful home truths that we in the audience aren't allowed to hear, eyes roll, bodies totter, and I wound up every bit as angry at Mr. Wyler as I was at the nasty little brat who started all the trouble." *Time* was even less charitable: "But much of the film is

In a scene with her *Charade* co-star, Cary Grant, Hepburn once again dresses in simple but elegant style.

directed . . . on the assumption that the perceptive level of the audience is that of a roomful of producers' relatives. Audrey Hepburn, the other teacher, gives her standard frail, indomitable characterization, which is to say that her eyes water constantly (frailty) and her chin is forever cantilevered forward (indomitability). Little is asked of James (*Maverick*) Garner, and he gives it."

Perhaps it was the relative failure of *The Children's Hour* that caused Hepburn to agree to make two more films in quick succession. Both were shot on location in Paris, starting late in 1962 and continuing into early 1963. The movie shot first was *Paris When It Sizzles*, which was shelved for two years after it was completed; it was not released until 1964. Therefore it was *Charade*, the second film to be shot, that was the first to be released.

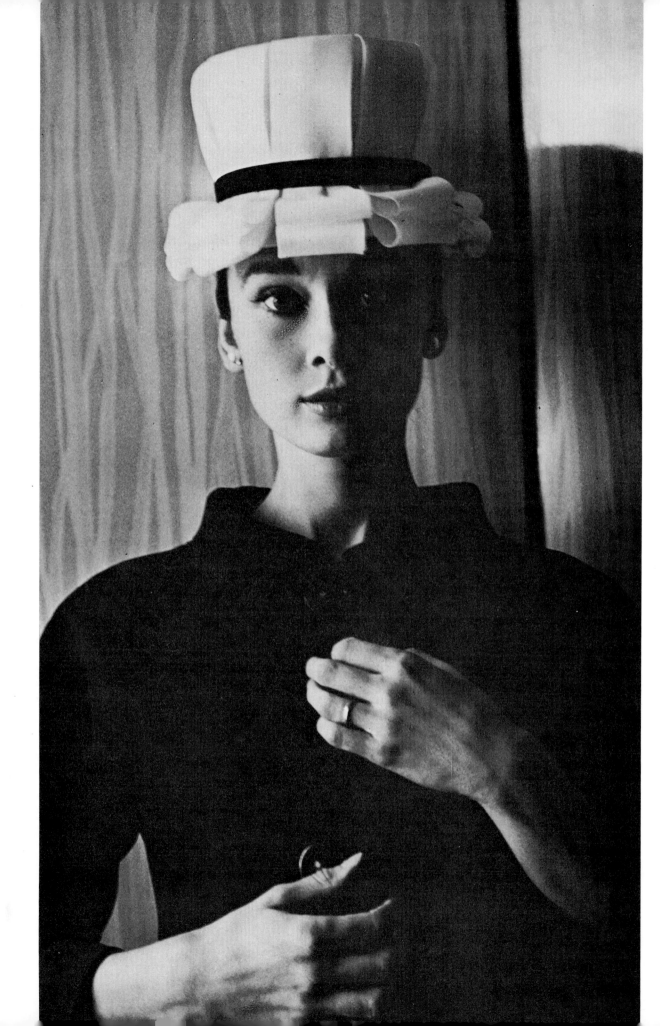

Charade at last gave Hepburn the chance to costar with the seemingly elusive Cary Grant, who had so frequently been proposed as her leading man by Billy Wilder. But this time he was not the beneficiary; rather it was Stanley Donen who directed the film for Universal. Critics agree in labelling it the best of Donen's non-musical films.

The screenplay for *Charade* was written by Peter Stone and based on a story he had written with Marc Behm called "The Unsuspecting Wife." The tone of the screenplay is clearly Hitchcockian in its origins and therefore invites comparisons with other comedy/thriller/romances from the hand of the master. Although some critics have pointed out that Hitchcock might have made more of some of the bits of business, it is hard to see how even he could have made a more successful film. John Baxter has pointed out that *Charade* itself led to a flock of imitations, among them *Mirage*, *Masquerade*, Donen's own *Arabesque*, *Kaleidoscope*, *Caprice* and *Blindfold*.

Charade opens with seemingly wealthy and socially well-connected Regina Lambert (Hepburn) on a skiing vacation at a Swiss resort. When she finally returns to her Paris apartment, she finds that her husband has been murdered and the furnishings of her apartment have completely vanished. Confused and without immediate resource, she accepts the offer of help from a handsome stranger she met in Switzerland, Peter Joshua (Cary Grant). But she continues to be pursued by a gang of thieves, evidently attempting to get from her the $250,000 it is believed her husband has stolen. Several plot twists and a few gruesome murders later, Regina has become suspicious of both Peter's motives and his identity, so attempts on her own to go to the American Embassy for help. The man she meets there (Walter Matthau, before he started to be a lovable curmudgeon) encourages her suspicions about Peter and urges her to try to uncover the whereabouts of the missing money. She finally discovers that her husband had invested his ill-gotten gains in a single rare stamp, and of course her discovery of that stamp sets up the long tense final scene that begins with her attempt to escape from Peter, and progresses to what seems like the climax as she must make a quick choice — her life literally depends on it — between Peter and the man from the Embassy. But her correct choice of Peter only leads to one more chase, as she plays a deadly game of cat-and-mouse in an empty theater, hunted by the man who isn't really from the Embassy at all. But Peter saves her, and all that's left is a final twist as she (and the audience) discovers Peter's true identity (a benign secret, naturally) and the fade-out clinch.

The mood of *Charade* is established in the very first shot of the film. Audrey Hepburn (Givenchy'd up, as usual) is seen sunning herself at Megève, a picture of unsuspecting serenity. Suddenly, the camera picks up a gun, emerging from a mysteriously gloved hand, aimed straight at Hepburn's head. The trigger is pulled and SPLASH! Hepburn's ear is full of water as we suddenly understand she is the victim of nothing more sinister than a prank with a child's water pistol. Throughout the movie, Donen continues to surprise us with his quick shifts from one mood to the other, his deft handling of the surprises in the script.

Charade is often genuinely tense, and there is a high incidence of real death. But the villains are just exaggerated enough to be a little

Certainly a departure from her avowed belief in

simple hats!

amusing: George Kennedy with a murderous hook replacing one hand, and James Coburn whose "jest-folks-from-Texas" act covers an extreme viciousness. We shudder when they close in on the heroine, but Donen manages to make us laugh at their own grisly demises.

Charade ranked Number 5 at the box office for the year, grossing more than $6,000,000. Contemporary reviews seemed a bit grudging in their praise. The movie was too easy, too slick, too Hollywood for them to be comfortable with their enjoyment. Philip Hartung, for example, admitted that Stanley Donen succeeded in "holding your attention with his good cast, engaging shots of off-beat Paris, and amusing give-and-take between Cary Grant and Audrey Hepburn, both of whom are fine in the give-and-take department," but he also complained that "you begin to suspect the picture is working overtime to keep you mystified." What?! They want you to have a good time?!

Richard Whitehall said that the film failed to "link the comic and the macabre into a stylistic unity," but he commended the witty dialogue, the beautifully choreographed and filmed chase sequences, and the performances of the stars: "Hepburn, an elegant apparition in her Givenchy gowns, gives her usual distinctive performance, but Grant, skillfully handling some of the best material he's worked on in a long time, comes up with one of his happiest high-comedy performances." *Newsweek* was apparently less troubled by the slickness of *Charade*, calling it "an absolute delight in which Cary Grant and Audrey Hepburn schottische about with evident glee." One of the film's greatest fans was Pauline Kael, who wrote sardonically, "I couldn't persuade friends to go see *Charade*, which although no more than a charming confectionary trifle, was, I think, probably the best American film of last year — as artificial and enjoyable in its way as *The Big Sleep*. The word has got around that it isn't *important*, that it isn't *serious*, that it doesn't do anything for you." Luckily, a lot of people in the country were *not* Pauline Kael's friends . . .

Charade received no Academy Award nominations, but Hepburn did win Actress of the Year from the British Film Institute. It is to be hoped that this consoled her for the critical reception of her next film to be released, *Paris When It Sizzles*. On paper, the project sounds like a good one. The screenplay was written by George Axelrod. The concept was based on a 1955 French film, written and directed by Julien Duvivier, that starred Hildegard Knef and Michel Auclair. Hepburn's co-star was once again William Holden, and she had another Givenchy wardrobe to gladden the eyes of fashion-conscious viewers. Noel Coward played a supporting role, and Marlene Dietrich, Tony Curtis, and Mel Ferrer all played cameo parts. The whole thing was set and filmed in beautiful Paris. What more does any movie need?

Well, for one thing, a better script. For another, some crisp and strong direction. A leading man better suited to the part might have helped too.

In *Paris When It Sizzles,* Hepburn had the chance to play many heroines in brief vignettes; here she is in a World War I flying sequence.

The premise of *Paris When It Sizzles* seems to lend itself to a wide realm of possibilities. Screenwriter Richard Benson (William Holden) has failed to apply himself to his current assignment, writing a screenplay for a world-famous producer (Noel Coward), and so the producer visits him in high dudgeon to demand a finished product in 48 hours. Panic-stricken, the writer drafts his typist Gabrielle (Hepburn) into helping him with his monumental task. On this framework is set a number of vignettes that are the raw material of the imagined script, acted out by the frantic pair of writers. There are comedy bits, spy thriller moments, snatches of musicals, and anything else they can dredge up. By the time the deadline is at hand, they have fallen in love, and although there is a temporary separation (to show you the imaginative level of the script, the writer declares he is not worthy of Gabrielle) they are reunited in a happy ending that also somehow manages to imply what is even more unlikely – that a decent script will somehow emerge from all this.

The reviews of this leaden confection were deadly. Stanley Kauffman said, "Axelrod simply flounders. His dialogue and Holden's gift for comedy amply deserve each other. Noel Coward is briefly on hand at his most repellent. And in the midst of this meager harvest is Miss Audrey Hepburn, trying to make chaff out of corn." Hollis Alpert, writing for *Saturday Review*, lambasts, "Fatuous is perhaps the word that best describes the quality of the writing. One would hardly expect, then, that Miss Hepburn or Mr. Holden would be able to surmount the handicap of their basic material, and they do not. Their pretense of a light kidding style is simply bad acting and (I guess)

bad direction . . . a dreadfully expensive display of bad taste." The *New York Times* was slightly more charitable: "Miss Hepburn, sylphlike as ever, seems slightly bewildered by the trumped-up zaniness in which she is involved . . . In their breathless efforts at making *Paris* fashionable, smart, and 'in,' Mr. Axelrod and Mr. Quine and their stars are not really inventive or funny." Judith Crist opined, "Miss Hepburn is, as always, very lovely to look at and so is Paris. Mr. Holden, however, is not Cary Grant, even though he tries and he tries and he tries. And *Paris When It Sizzles*? Strictly Hollywood — when it fizzles." Perhaps the snidest remark came from a critic who was amused to note that the credits cited Givenchy for Hepburn's wardrobe *and* perfume. He remarked that the perfume couldn't be smelled but the picture could.

In line with the pattern of one hit and one miss that seemed to be establishing itself for Hepburn in the Sixties, she followed up this rather lame film with one that was a critical box office success. It was *My Fair Lady*, made by Warner Brothers and released in 1964. She won the plum role of Eliza Doolittle.

Her selection came as something of a surprise in Hollywood. Many people had assumed that the creator of the role in the stage version of the musical, Julie Andrews, would get the part. But producer Jack Warner felt that she was not a big enough star. He was determined to have Hepburn, and he was quoted as saying that her participation in the film would guarantee at least $5 million in additional box office receipts. So he offered her a contract for one million dollars. (Only three other stars had yet reached this pinnacle: Marlon Brando, Elizabeth Taylor, and Sophia Loren.) When you add to this the $5.5 million that Warner had already paid to get the movie rights to the musical, you can see that *My Fair Lady* was destined to be a big-budget production.

Total costs did in fact mount to well over $15 million. Part of that was in salaries. Rex Harrison was hired to recreate the role of Henry Higgins, and you can bet he didn't come cheap. Supporting cast members included Stanley Holloway, Wilfrid Hyde-White, Gladys Cooper, Theodore Bikel, and Mona Washbourne. George Cukor was hired to direct, and Alan Jay Lerner, who wrote the book for the Broadway show, was asked to do the screenplay. (Just for good measure, Warner also bought the rights to the 1938 film version of *Pygmalion*, the George Bernard Shaw play on which *My Fair Lady* is based.) Hermes Pan was engaged as the choreographer for the ballroom sequences, and Cecil Beaton designed the costumes as well as some of the lavish sets. Andre Previn adapted the Lerner and Loewe songs for use in the movie and added incidental music. Warner Brothers seemed determined to spare no expense.

Perhaps one reason that Jack Warner was so certain Audrey Hepburn was right for the role of Eliza is that *My Fair Lady* boils down to one more version of the Cinderella story. Eliza Doolittle is a lower-class girl who sells flowers outside Covent Garden. She accosts Professor Henry Higgins (Rex Harrison) and his friend Colonel Pickering (Wilfrid Hyde-White) one evening in an attempt to make a sale, and their conversation leads to a wager by Higgins that he can use his skill in linguistics to teach even a Cockney

At the beginning of *My Fair Lady*, Hepburn had to appear plastered with dirt, her hair caked with soil, as the Cockney flower-seller — Cinderella before the fairy godmother.

guttersnipe like Eliza to speak so much like a lady that no one in accent-conscious London will be able to guess her origins. So Eliza goes off to live in Higgins' house and begin her transformation. Of course, she needs to learn much more than simply how to speak correctly, and she occasionally rebels at the strenuousness of her training. But at last her tutor judges her ready for the great imposture, and he introduces her to society at a ball — where she does indeed pass careful inspection by haughty English aristocrats. Her initial appearance is followed by several more social triumphs, and she begins to fancy herself in love with a callow but titled youth (Jeremy Brett). But after a blazing argument with Higgins that causes her to leave his roof, both transformer and transformed realize they have fallen in love, and they are reunited at last.

Hepburn's great disappointment in playing Eliza was that she was not allowed to do her own singing as she had originally been promised. It was eventually decided to dub in Marni Nixon's voice, to which Hepburn lip-synched, and this destroyed some of the charm and spontaneity of her performance. Gary Carey has remarked in his book on Cukor, "The ubiquitous Marni Nixon supplied the colorless Jeanette MacDonald soprano that rings from Miss Hepburn's lips. Frederick Loewe's music is not so sacrosanct that it needs this kind of hallowed operetta-ish respect. If Harrison could deliver his songs in an Americanized recitative, there is no reason why Hepburn shouldn't deliver hers in her own humanly vulnerable voice."

But generally, the experience was a pleasant one. Hepburn enjoyed working with Cukor, who returned the sentiment; he said of her, "She's a hard worker . . . extremely intelligent, inventive, modest . . . and funny. To work with her you wouldn't think she was this great star. She's tactful, the most endearing creature in the world." Rex Harrison called her a sweet and gentle person and said he thought she gave a superb performance. Beaton, who wrote a book about his experience in trying to bring the sets and costumes to life, spoke of his enjoyment in creating her wardrobe, and certainly she does look especially ravishing in all the fancy-dress scenes.

Oddly enough, one of the few negative responses to Hepburn's performance concerned her appearance. Several critics remarked that she seemed a bit old for the obviously girlish role, and Henry Hart commented, "One of the most poignant things I have yet seen on the screen is youth being simulated by acting art on Miss Hepburn's face — amid those particular wrinkles which first announce that youth is over." Since Hepburn was then 35, it is not surprising that she had finally outgrown girlishness, but *My Fair Lady* brought the first public recognition of the fact.

In general the reviews were good. The box office repaid Warner Brothers' extravagance in production. And the awards were gratifying. *My Fair Lady* won the Oscar as Best Picture of the Year (also the New York Film Critics Award, the Golden Globe, and the British Academy Award.) Harrison was chosen by the American Academy and the New York Film Critics. Cukor won the Oscar and a Golden Globe for Best Director. In all, the picture won seven American Academy Awards, and even more nominations:

When the filming of *My Fair Lady* was over, Audrey Hepburn sent Cecil Beaton a little note thanking him for making her look so beautiful. The costumes were ravishing.

Stanley Holloway and Gladys Cooper for Best Supporting Actor and Actress; Alan Jay Lerner for Screenplay; Cecil Beaton for costumes.

Conspicuous by her absence from every single nomination list was Hepburn. Rex Harrison said he thought it was because it was widely known that her singing had been dubbed. Others have suggested that movie professionals thought it was somehow unfair for her to have taken the role from Julie Andrews — who ironically did win the Best Actress Oscar for her role in *Mary Poppins*. It may also have been due in part to the fact that Eliza is a somewhat unrealistic creation who must go from ragamuffin to lady of fashion before our generally disbelieving eyes. It was generally agreed that Hepburn was excellent in the latter part of the film, but many found her unconvincing as the grubby Cockney flowerseller. (An interesting sidelight that may emphasize her subliminal unsuitability for the early demands of the role: when she was costumed in Eliza's seedy rags, her hair caked with dirt and oil, mud even carefully plastered under her fingernails, Hepburn insisted on spraying herself with $100-an-ounce Joy to keep up her morale.)

Her fellow professionals were very supportive. Rex Harrison said publicly that he thought she should have been nominated for an award, and when he won his Oscar (she happened to be the presenter) he commented that he wished he could split it in half to share with her. Veteran Katharine Hepburn sent her a kind telegram that said, "Don't worry about not being nominated. Some day you'll get another one for a part that doesn't rate."

For consolation, Hepburn's next film gave her a chance again to work with William Wyler. Shooting began in the late fall of 1965, in Paris, on *How To Steal A Million*. It fits in the genre that might be called comedy caper, similar to *The Pink Panther*, Blake Edwards' recent hit, or the earlier *Topkapi*. Although the plot has certain elements that make it similar to *Charade*, the chief difference is that in *How To Steal A Million*, we are never really worried about the fate of the heroine. The happy ending is always visible just around the corner.

Hepburn's role is that of the charming daughter of an art forger (Hugh Griffith) who has gotten rich on his fake Renoirs and van Goghs. She is concerned that his imprudent behavior will lead to his unmasking, especially when he offers to allow a museum to exhibit his so-called Cellini statue, actually a fake made by his father, the first forger in the family. While he is out celebrating this coup one night, Hepburn catches what she supposes to be a burglar (Peter O'Toole) trying to steal one of the fake van Goghs. She accidentally shoots him in the arm, and according to Hollywood convention, this leads to a warmer acquaintance. When Hepburn and her father learn that the museum will conduct authentication tests on the statue (for insurance purposes) Hepburn hatches a scheme to steal it from a museum before it can be revealed as a fake. She therefore enlists O'Toole's help. (By this time, the audience has learned that he is actually an art detective already on her father's trail, but Hepburn still supposes him to be a burglar.) After the shortest planning period in modern cinematic history, they pull off the caper in an extended scene that is amusing and romantic — they are shut up in close

In her dressing room on the set of *Charade*, Hepburn

sits with her Yorkshire terrier, Assam. He was the

reason she liked her coats to be reversible: "When

the dog jumps on it and makes a spot, I just wear the

other side."

proximity in a tiny broom closet for hours — rather than thrilling. Once the caper has been satisfactorily executed, all that remains is to tie up a few loose ends: O'Toole reveals his true identity and warns her father to stop his nefarious activities, Hepburn breaks her engagement (entered into inadvertantly) to a crazed American art collector (Eli Wallach) and O'Toole gives him the fake statue, knowing he will keep it safe from prying eyes. Then the lovers can drive off to catch a plane for their honeymoon (although as they leave, we see that her father is, in fact, still up to his old tricks).

Critics attacked *How To Steal A Million* for being little more than an extended appreciation of Audrey Hepburn. Despite O'Toole's charming performance, the movie never seems quite as interesting as Audrey herself. In fact, the absorption with Hepburn's looks and mannerisms often teeters on the edge of parody. When we first see her, she is wearing a Givenchy suit, close-fitting hat, and huge bug-eye sunglasses; the look is so extremely stylish it is virtually repellent. In the scene where she wakes up in the middle of the night to find O'Toole burglarizing the living room, there is not the slightest effort made to suggest some altered bedtime state. She *is* wearing a nightgown, but her hair is still carefully teased into its helmet shape and her eyes are ringed with their customary heavy eyeliner and mascara. Even the dialogue occasionally refers to Hepburn rather than to the forger's daughter. When O'Toole disguises her in a cleaning woman's shabby dress, he says, "That does it!" "Does what?" she asks. "Well, for one thing, it gives Givenchy a night off."

There's always a certain point in the career of a successful movie star in which the personal legend begins to swamp any mere character in a movie. The star (and the star's directors) are then faced with the problem of how to use this powerful image. One solution is to limit the star's appearance to roles that more or less replicate the personal image. This, for example, has been the case with Katharine Hepburn, who plays a doughtily independent and high-minded woman over and over. Another possibility is gently to mock the legend, using audience memories of the star's previous films as an implicit contrast. An example is John Wayne in *True Grit*, attacking a gang of bad guys single-handed (and single-eyed) at a full gallop on his poor winded horse, the reins between his teeth, firing one shotgun and simultaneously cocking the other over his shoulder. In his younger days, such a scene would have been rejected as unbelievable; now our memories of all those bad guys he had faced down makes us laugh comfortably at this overblown spectacle.

In *How To Steal A Million*, Audrey Hepburn and her director William Wyler (who had something to do with the creation of her legend) seem to have chosen something closer to the second course. We get a hint — no more than that, but unmistakeably a hint — that there is something the tiniest bit ridiculous about all that elaborate chic, that relentless high-style grooming.

Interestingly, Hepburn's next picture moved her away from haute couture chic and into plastic earrings and Paco Rabanne clothes made of shiny metal disks. News of this fashion development almost overshadowed reviews of the movie itself.

Hepburn tries on her wardrobe; bending over at the right of the photo is Givenchy.

Two For the Road was produced and directed by Stanley Donen, who obviously had Hepburn in mind for his heroine from the start. But she had reservations. The script, written by Frederic Raphael (who had the recent hit, *Darling*, to his credit) included an adulterous affair, an appearance in a bathing suit, and a sizzling bedroom scene wearing nothing at all. Hepburn was afraid both that the picture would offend her fans and that she would be unable to give a convincing performance. But her husband urged her to go ahead with it, and she finally agreed.

The story of *Two For the Road* is a simple one. It's about a couple (Hepburn and Albert Finney) who meet, marry and adjust. We see them at five different stages during the twelve years of their relationship, always when they are traveling in France. They meet when she is a student traveling with a bus-load of giggling girls and he is a hitchhiker looking at great old buildings. (He is studying architecture.) Shortly thereafter, we see them as newly-weds, sharing a car with a ghastly older couple (Eleanor Bron and William Daniels) and their obnoxious child. A few years later, they are young marrieds with an elderly and unreliable MG. Then he begins to have some success in his profession, and they have a Triumph Herald — and a sagging marriage that leads to bitter arguments and infidelities. Our final view of the couple shows them to be prosperous (in a Mercedes 230) and "adjusted;" that is, they know one another's bad points but still choose to remain together.

The chronology of this capsule summary is not that of the film. Donen cuts back and forth through these five stages of the couple's relationship using a seamless flashback technique that gives no indication of the changing time. The viewer must sort things out on his own, using the cars, the clothes, and the state of the relationship as clues. When the tech-

nique works, it evokes the close scrutiny of the couple that the director desires; when it fails, it simply confuses (or bores) the audience. Critics were evenly divided as to which occurred more frequently.

Pauline Kael called the movie a good try, although she thought Finney and Hepburn made an odd couple. Flavia Wharton, in *Films in Review*, called the movie "soapera" and accused Hepburn of "prostituting her very genuine acting abilities on behalf of a script designed by Frederic Raphael exclusively for feeble female minds." *Life* suggested that the film might be "a turning point for the upper-class commercial movie," but *Newsweek* griped that "Hepburn's many time-spanning costume changes . . . and Finney's progression of flashy sports cars help mark the passage of time but fail to make up for the basic disharmony." Brendan Gill said the stars are "among the best-looking and most appealing performers on earth . . . but oh, what unpleasant roles they are called upon to enact!" He concluded that "the grim message of the film – the only thing worse than spending a lifetime with another person is to spend a lifetime alone – makes an uncomfortable basis for the slick and debonaire comedy that Mr. Donen evidently had it in mind to give us." *Saturday Review* termed the film "diverting enough if not sensationally enjoyable," but *Films and Filming* raved that "the picture is a combination of American expertise and European cool. It is charming, scintillating and flashy, but it contains enough depth and recognisable moments, those secret intimate moments which everyone thinks of as his private property, that the film is satisfying on many levels."

Some of the contemporary press coverage was devoted to the fact that Hepburn was not – gasp! – dressed by Givenchy for this film. Instead, many of her outfits (by Mary Quant, Paco Rabanne, and Michele Rosier) came off the rack from trendy London boutiques, and the rest of her wardrobe was designed by the light-hearted young American, Ken Scott. There was also much talk about the exposure of her legs in very short skirts and her decolletage in a bathing suit, and the fact that the script called for her to be frequently in bed with Albert Finney was also the subject of some comment. In all of this, we see another example of the film using a star's legend as part of the subtext. It is the audience's knowledge of Hepburn's ladylike image that makes *Two For the Road* seem shockingly contemporary. For example, had the role been played by Julie Christie or Jeanne Moreau, actresses whose screen persona already included a large measure of amorality, the wife's infidelity would not have seemed so obvious a sign of the marriage's troubles. Another way in which Hepburn herself is used in the character of Joanna is through our shared recollection of her youthful image. Neither the makeup nor the script is completely successful in evoking the young Joanna, with her innocent gaity and idealism, but the failure doesn't matter because Hepburn's mere presence conjures up all those young heroines of her past, and we willingly read those qualities into the space Donen and scriptwriter James Goldman have left us.

Hepburn's next film was her last of the decade of the Sixties. It was produced by her husband for Warner Brothers, who had bought the movie rights to the successful Broadway play written by Frederick Knotts

This charming little lacy veil is Hepburn's disguise as she plots a crime in *How To Steal A Million*.

(who also wrote the screenplay of Hitchcock's *Dial M For Murder*). On stage, the lead had been played by Lee Remick, but of course Hepburn was considered a better box office draw for a film. The property was *Wait Until Dark*, and Hepburn had the challenging role of a blind woman menaced by a group of thieves. The plot of *Wait Until Dark* has all the tension and uncertainty of *Charade*, but this time there is no comic relief, no blooming romance to lighten the atmosphere — and the heroine has the extra handicap of blindness thrown in for good measure.

The heroine of the movie is Suzy Hendrix, a young woman recently blinded in an accident. Her husband (Efrem Zimbalist, Jr.) who does his best to encourage her self-sufficiency, is a photographer who has been traveling on assignment. Returning through customs, he is given a doll by a fellow passenger; we quickly learn this is an expedient for getting the dope-laden doll in the country. As soon as he returns to their Greenwich Village apartment and deposits the doll, he is lured away. The gang of smugglers then attempt to get the doll from his wife. Their strategy involves a series of impostures, which the audience gradually uncovers. Alan Arkin plays the archvillain, turning up in a variety of disguises. Jack Weston pretends to be a cop, and most convincing of all, Richard Crenna pretends to be an old Army buddy of the photographer. The conspirators grow increasingly desperate and begin knocking one another off, and by the tense finale of the film, only Arkin is left, his villainy out in the open as he attempts to kill Hepburn. She evens the odds by turning out the lights, and the hair-raising climax takes place in the dark. Just as it is all over, the photographer comes home, the lights go on, and the audience exhales in relief as they discover Hepburn alive and well.

It is not easy to play a blind person convincingly, especially without the disguise of dark glasses, but Hepburn does it extremely well. She spent some time at an Institute for the Blind in Switzerland preparing for the role, and she seems to have been a careful observer. Her performance brought her another Academy Award nomination, her fifth, although she lost to the sentimental favorite, Katharine Hepburn in *Guess Who's Coming to Dinner*.

The film was generally very well reviewed. The *New York Morning Telegraph* called Hepburn's portrayal of the heroine "highly appealing" and predicted "you'll find your fingernails chewed down to the elbow when the lights come on again at the end of the film." Andrew Sarris complained about some of the plot implausibilities — one of them being the fact that Arkin disguises himself in fake moustaches and wigs to deceive a blind woman — but concludes that "the film is redeemed . . . by a surprise stroke of terror that should made audiences gasp and scream from Radio City Music Hall to Rangoon." *Variety* predicted (correctly) that it would have a hot box office — it turned out to be Number 13 in gross receipts at the end of the year — and went on to say that "Aided by the generally strong script, Miss Hepburn conveys superbly the combination of helplessness and sense acuity sometimes found in the blind."

Wait Until Dark was released in the fall of 1967. It would be nearly ten years before Audrey Hepburn made another film.

This picture of Audrey Hepburn and Mel Ferrer was

taken not long before they separated.

Recent Work

When Hepburn finished shooting *Wait Until Dark*, she made a formal announcement of her separation from Mel Ferrer. She soon followed that up by filing for divorce. It became final over a year later, in December of 1968.

It appears that the marriage, despite the good intentions and best efforts of both parties, was a victim of the show business syndrome. Hepburn's career went too far, too fast, while Ferrer's seemed to be slipping down from its never very lofty peak. An article critical of Hepburn (written before the separation) seemed to sum up a prevailing view of the relationship; "When it started out, there were those accusing Mel of being the duo's Svengali – the guy who was calling the turns and influencing Audrey in all her demands and insistence on the status symbol of a superstar. The years between have changed that conception of the marriage quite considerably. It's pretty obvious that Audrey has been in the driver's seat from the beginning. She seems happy keeping busy and Mel looks well fed and comfortable as a here-today, gone-tomorrow husband, who for the past several years has managed to keep oceans between himself and his wife."

But it seems obvious that Ferrer's attitude toward the situation was not really so complacent. He gave an interview shortly before the separation in which he complained of the humiliation of knowing that many people who called him to talk about a script were really just trying to find a way to get to Audrey, and offers of work to him were sometimes merely a bait to get Hepburn to sign up. Feeling bitter and undermined, he began to appear openly with other women. Hepburn herself was rumored to be having an affair with co-star William Holden. The handwriting was on the wall, despite several reconciliation attempts.

Robin and Marian (1976) was the first appearance of the new, softer Audrey Hepburn.

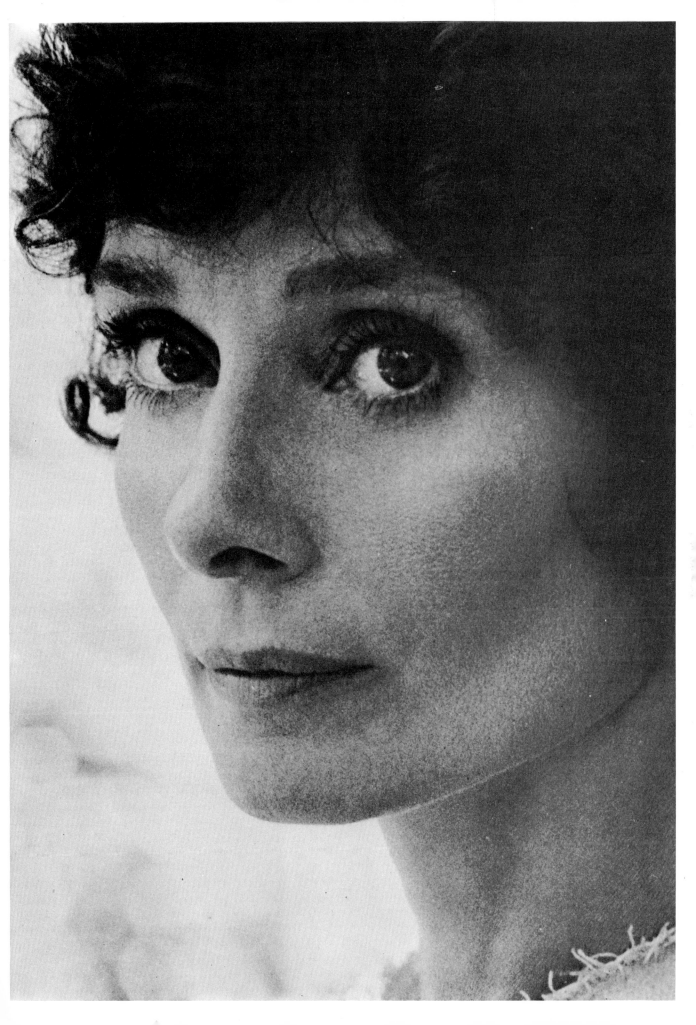

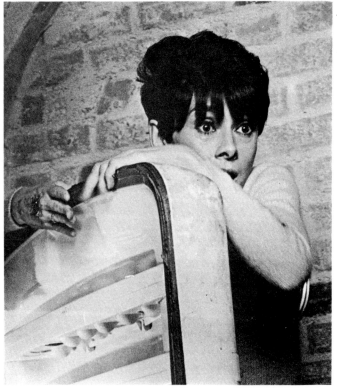

△ Hepburn relaxes with her husband, Dr Andrea Dotti, and her son, Sean Ferrer.

▷ At the heart-stopping climax of *Wait Until Dark*, Audrey Hepburn is revealed to the anxious audience to be alive and well as she emerges from the hiding place behind the refrigerator door.

While Hepburn was waiting for the divorce to become final, she met and fell in love with the man who was to become her second husband. He was Dr. Andrea Dotti, an Italian psychiatrist who was practicing in Switzerland. The son of a Milanese industrialist, Dotti was socially prominent and a frequent extra man on the guest lists of international society hostesses. He and Hepburn got to know one another as fellow guests on the yacht of Princess Olimpia Torlonia and her husband Paul Weiller (son of the French petrol magnate) during a cruise of the Greek Islands. When the cruise ended, Hepburn returned quietly to Switzerland but continued to see Dotti with as little publicity as possible. During the Christmas season of 1968, after Hepburn's divorce was final, Dotti gave her an engagement ring from Bulgaria, and they were married in Switzerland the following month.

Once again, Hepburn settled down to be a wife and mother. Her son Sean Ferrer lived with them, and another son, Luca, was added to the family in 1970. They bought a Swiss villa, and Hepburn exercised considerable creativity in furnishing it and creating a cozy domestic environment. In rare interviews, she always spoke about his career rather than hers: "When you are in love, you become madly interested in anything your husband does, even shoemaking, and Andrea's work is especially involving . . . But he also needs desperately to relax. Of all branches of medicine, his is one of the most emotionally trying and draining." Obviously she considered it her mission to provide the atmosphere in which this much-needed relaxation was possible. Hepburn frequently denied that she had "retired," but the years of involvement with home and family slipped away. She did not return to her own work until 1976 – amid rumors that her husband was constantly seen with other women and the marriage was foundering.

The film that marked her return to the screen after an absence of nearly a decade was *Robin and Marian*. Apparently, she had seen the script several years earlier and decided that she wanted to do the film, but waited patiently while producer Ray Stark assembled the rest of the cast. That persuasive screenplay was by James Goldman, who had won an Oscar in 1968 for *The Lion in Winter*, which had starred Katharine Hepburn and Peter O'Toole. *Robin and Marian* had obvious similarities in its treatment of the relationship of an older couple who hold sway over a group of assembled courtiers. There is also a similarity of tone — elegant, ironic, poetical – that is contrasted with the occasional bite of down-to-earth recognition of reality.

The story of *Robin and Marian* is an imaginative sequel to the familiar tale that always seems to end with the pair's happy clinch. Goldman hypothesizes that shortly after Robin (Sean Connery) and Marian (Hepburn) settle down to live happily ever after, he goes off to crusade with King Richard the Lion-Heart (Richard Harris). After twenty years of fighting, Richard turns mean and a little mad and finally is killed by an arrow *thrown* at him by an angry little old man. Disillusioned, Robin and Little John (Nicol Williamson) return to England. There Robin discovers that Marian has entered a convent and become the Abbess. He rescues her from anti-clerical persecution, and their romance begins all over again. Robin finds a new challenge in attempting once more to help the people who are oppressed by

King John (Ian Holm) and the Sheriff of Nottingham (Robert Shaw). But although the re-assembled band does pull off one glorious escapade, it becomes obvious that Robin is physically too old and spiritually too uncertain to succeed in such a mission. The loving Marian comes up with the ultimate solution: she gives Robin poison and then drinks it herself — thus setting free the power of the legend.

Robin and Marian is really a story about loss. First it raises the question of whether the personal sacrifice, the deaths, the cruel demands of the long crusade have been worth it, as Robin returns home to see the ideals he fought for progressively more debased. Then the movie deals with the more personal theme of lost time in Robin and Marian's relationship. The love and happiness and trust of their youth is unrecoverable, no matter how much they may still love one another; with their poignant realization of that fact, they are able to go on and make the best of what they do have.

In the role of Marian, Hepburn at last plays the part of a fully mature woman who is perfectly capable of being responsible for her own destiny. Scriptwriter Goldman indirectly commented on the departure this represented from her typical roles; "It would be interesting to know why Marian appealed to Audrey. You know, in her former roles, she always played the innocent woman who had been swept up by circumstances rather than her own choices. As Marian, she seduces herself. It is Marian who chooses to go back to Robin after all these years, to give up her religious vows and return to the uncertainty and the brawling. Marian is a strong woman with a determined will and yet impulsively emotional — it's not what one expects of Audrey's image."

When the reporter put that question to Hepburn, her answer emphasized that she had knowingly opted to play a fully mature woman. She said, "I had a flash when I read the script. I never lost that excitement. I feel it is important. There's a great need in films today for mature women to be seen playing mature women. And this was one of the few stories where I could be my own age. I like that."

Most critics felt that she was perfectly cast as Marian, and the fact that she, like her character, was a gracefully aging legend heightened her effectiveness in the role. Frank Rich commented on this connection. "Miss Hepburn's performance is also an elucidation of her old screen persona. She isn't a gamine any more, though she looks at least a decade younger than her actual age (46); her classic facial planes have become softer, and her wispy cosmopolitan voice has been filled out by heartier, deeper chords; even her hair has more texture than it did before. She's still an elegant woman, but you feel (especially in a comic scene where she asks Robin about the women he's had during their separation) that she's been around far more than even Holly Golightly had been. At the same time, when she breaks into sobs over the possibility that Robin might be taken from her again, she seems the essence of human fragility. Hepburn can take us from autumn to spring and back again in two minutes — she's a genuine miracle."

Despite the outstanding cast and excellent script, Robin and Marian is a flawed movie. One reason may have been the direction of Richard

With co-star Sean Connery in Robin and Marian, she made us believe in a mature love story.

Lester, best known for his jerky, high-energy movies of the Sixties – the Beatles movies, *The Knack*, the more recent *Three Musketeers*. Some members of the cast and crew complained that he was driving through the filming too fast, relying too much on impromptu inspiration, and especially too prone to make hasty decisions to add some slapstick bit of business – thereby undermining the thoughtfulness and emotional impact of the screenplay. Hepburn commented tactfully, "I've never made a film so fast and I would like to have had more time. But he [Lester] is very different – extraordinary, spontaneous. Everything had to be new, practically impromptu." A studio executive amplified, "Audrey could get along with Hitler, but Lester is not high in her scrapbook of unforgettable characters." One other reason for the film's shortcomings may be that during the filming the picture moved somewhat away from the original concept toward a more action-oriented movie. This trend probably reflected both Lester's own tendencies and experience, and the collective influence of that large and very talented male cast that he had to work with. Hepburn said she had to fight to retain the romantic scenes between Robin and Marian; "With all those men, I was the one who had to defend the romance in the picture. Somebody had to take care of Marian."

The reviews were all very favorable to Hepburn, making it clear that her return to the screen was no disappointment. But opinion about the success of the movie was by no means so unanimous. Several critics agreed that Hepburn's instinctive attempt to emphasize the love story was correct. Vincent Canby said, "*Robin and Marian* is at its best when it plays its

love story without smart talk or gags, largely through Miss Hepburn's magnificent face, which time has touched just enough to make us aware of the waste that Marian's last 20 years represent . . . The strength of *Robin and Marian*, which was once titled *The Death of Robin and Marian*, is in its story about two former lovers who discover – in themselves and in each other – something new, more valuable than what had existed before."

Shortly after the film was released, Hepburn and Dotti agreed to end their marriage. There was little publicity, and Hepburn continued to live quietly with her two sons. But the lessened domestic demands made her more able and more willing to work, and so it wasn't long until she signed to do another movie. She was approached by Terence Hill, her director in *Wait Until Dark,* who had become a friend. His participation in the project was clearly one of the major reasons she agreed; perhaps a certain sense of familiarity about the script also inclined her to say yes. But it was a picture that looked backward to her earlier screen persona, rather than extending the new one she acquired in *Robin and Marian* – which is perhaps one reason it was so much less successful a venture.

The film, released in the summer of 1979, was *Bloodline*, a screen adaptation by Laird Koenig of Sidney Sheldon's best-selling novel. The part Hepburn plays, of Elizabeth Roffe, is a re-run of the role of Regina Lambert she had played fifteen years earlier in *Charade.* Once again, she is an innocent victim caught up in dangerous events that someone else has set in motion. Once again, she is seen in a dazzling variety of Givenchy outfits. But alas, there is no Cary Grant on the horizon, no comedy to lighten the atmosphere, and no cohesion to the over-complex plot.

Bloodline opens with the murder of the head of a prosperous family-owned pharmaceutical company. His daughter Elizabeth (Hepburn) inherits control, and then offends the rest of the family by her refusal to let the company go public. Soon, someone attempts to kill her so that her decision can be reversed. Is it her cousin (James Mason) who must pay the huge gambling debts of his pretty wife (Michelle Phillips)? Or her other cousin (Irene Papas) whose womanizing husband (Omar Sharif) is hungry for more money? Or her father's right-hand man (Ben Gazzara) who has his own ideas about the way the company should be run? Or her secretary (Beatrice Straight)? Or yet another cousin (calculating Romy Schneider) or her weak-willed husband (Maurice Ronet)? Then Elizabeth's secretary is murdered, and a detective (Gert Frobe) comes on the scene, using a computer to track down the villain (how we never understand). For reasons of business convenience – don't ask – Elizabeth agrees to marry the right-hand man, even though he is still a major suspect. After a few more twists and turns, mostly involving a subplot about porno snuff films, the movie abruptly finds its happy ending. Cousin James Mason is unmasked as the killer and Elizabeth falls into true love with her husband.

Most critics objected that the plot was preposterous and the script far too weak to sustain it. But Hepburn was certainly treated kindly. Derek Elley waxed nostalgic: "The ambit of the plot is Hepburn territory, sure enough, but the film as a whole is over-ridingly concerned with event rather

Audrey Hepburn at 50 is a much softened version of

her youthful self.

than character. Hepburn's supreme ability has always been to suffuse potentially shallow roles in glossy settings with real style and emotion, but in *Bloodline* she never stands a chance against the mass of the plot and other star-names all jostling for screen-time . . . There are odd moments – the walk in Central Park with Gazzara, or a scene alone in bed hoping the phone will ring – when the clock turns effortlessly back to Peppard and *Breakfast at Tiffany's*, even Holden and *Sabrina* . . . but then the plot closes in. This is not simple idle reminiscing: Hepburn gives ample proof of her unique magic still being there – it is just a crying shame to see it so squandered and underemployed. She still looks fabulous, moves gracefully, that special voice-color, guaranteed to make any Hepburnite's knees wobble at fifty paces, is as potent as ever; and she has an uncluttered dignity which puts even the impressive Romy Schneider firmly in the shade."

Another reminiscer was Stephen Saban in *The SoHo News*, who said, "Hepburn is a class act, a lady dressed in Givenchy. When she is in a scene, she makes all the men seem as urbane as Cary Grant and all the women as wooden as Ali MacGraw . . . Audrey Hepburn is always Audrey Hepburn – and thank god for that. What could be better? She makes all her lines sound as if they were out of *Charade*." Charles Sawyer was also nostalgic but less captivated: "Audrey Hepburn was excellent in *Wait Until Dark*, delightful in that terrible *Robin and Marian*, but in *Bloodline* she's a disappointment. As lovely as she is for a fiftyish woman, she's too old (and it shows) for this part. She still wears Givenchy like nobody else, but she's too classy a lady for such a coquettish performance."

Derek Elly closed his remarks by expressing the hope that "more works of the caliber of *Robin and Marian*, rather than faceless chic like *Bloodline*, will tempt her in the future." Unfortunately, that was not the case. Her next (and, as of this date, her last) movie was a vehicle of little distinction.

They All Laughed was directed by Peter Bogdanovich. The script, also written by him, is a silly tale of several private detectives and the ladies they are hired by jealous husbands to follow. The movie, much of it shot on location in New York, was released in the fall of 1981 and disappeared very quickly from first-run theaters, to a chorus of bad reviews. Heaven only knows what friendship induced Hepburn to appear in this one (there was a rumor that the attraction was a romance with her repeat co-star, Ben Gazzara, but if that was true she must have been doubly disappointed, as gossip from the set indicated they were on hostile terms by the end of the filming).

The plot, if you can call it that, of *They All Laughed*, revolves around the detective agency that employs John Russo (Ben Gazzara), Charles Rutledge (John Ritter, of TV's *Three's Company*) and Arthur Brodsky (played by the co-producer, Blaine Novak). For a period of one week (and it seems to take almost that long to sit through it) we watch them drifting around Manhattan, following the women they are paid to watch, as well as some they just happen to become involved with. Russo is shadowing Angela (Hepburn) the wife of an Italian industrialist, and for some inexplicable reason, by the middle of the movie they have fallen in love. Wandering through this farrago

The cast of *They All Laughed* included (l to r) Colleen Camp, Blaine Novak, Patti Hensen, Ben Gazzara, Audrey Hepburn, John Ritter, the late Dorothy Stratton, and George Morfogen.

are Colleen Camp playing a country-and-western singer, and model Patti Hansen playing the sexiest cabdriver you've ever seen. The film definitely has a home-movie touch, due to bit part appearances by Hepburn's son Sean and Bogdanovich's two daughters. The ending is either bittersweet or a return to good sense, depending on how you look at it. Angela dumps the detective (but tactfully, of course, on the grounds that duty calls.)

The reviews were not good. Although a critic at *The Village Voice* did claim, "It's a loving look at the bubbleheads who inhabit the Roxy and City Limits [two of New York's then hot night spots] everyone is dopey and jolly . . ." most writers seemed more impressed by the dopey aspect than the jolly one. Vincent Canby said, "Any way you look at it – as a comedy, as movie-making, as a financial investment, *They All Laughed* is an immodest disaster. It's aggressive in its ineptitude. It grates on the nerves like a 78 rpm record played at 33 rpm." *Newsweek* called the movie "an aimless bust, unencumbered by a visual or structural scheme. It wanders through a series of *boîtes*, boutiques and hotel lobbies in the vagrant hope of witnessing a privileged moment."

But Hepburn herself still pleased the viewers. One critic suggested sympathetically that Bogdanovich had treated her so badly that if it were a marriage instead of a movie, she'd have grounds for immediate divorce. *Newsweek*, trying for a balanced appraisal, said, "At 52, the eternal gamine has become a figure of icy chic; the lilt in her voice now has the gravity of years; she barely has a line to speak in the film's first hour, and too many silly words in the second. But she is still a radiant presence, and she blesses the end of *They All Laughed* with a display of poignant maturity. One would gladly pay to hear her read the Bel Air phone book."

It's undeniable that Hepburn's last two movies have been disappointing to her fans. But the problem has been the properties rather than the star. We can take comfort from the fact that her magic is obviously intact. No doubt her choice of roles is narrower now that she must play women "of a certain age" than it was earlier in her career, but there is every reason to hope that she will yet make more movies that will add to her legend and our memories.

Any movie star who has appeared on the screen for nearly thirty years acquires a powerful image. The accumulation of all those hours we've spent in cool, dim theaters leaves an indelible impression. We know the range of the voice, recognize the walk, anticipate the meaning of the slightest twitch of an eyebrow. Often our familiarity leads to a desire to imitate the star. This was especially true during the heydey of the big movie studio, with its corps of press agents who planted innumerable stories about the stars' taste in clothes, perfume, intimate apparel, and spouses. Even today, though, the magic prevails, and a movie like *Annie Hall* spurs thousands of young women to dress and do their hair like Diane Keaton.

But some stars have an impact even greater than the movie medium can explain, and one of those is Audrey Hepburn. The image of Hepburn is really part of our shared cultural experience. It has been a significant influence on the way women look, dress, and play the female role.

Our image of Hepburn is almost exclusively *visual*. It is based primarily on her movie appearances and secondarily on coverage in the fashion press of her personal wardrobe and style. Because she has chosen to keep her personal life as private as possible under the circumstances of superstardom, her popular image contains few "personality" traits. We think we know all about Elizabeth Taylor's weaknesses when it comes to men and food; or Doris Day's fabled love of home, children, and dogs; or Marilyn Monroe's troubled search for love. But few of us attach any such intimate characteristics to our picture of Audrey Hepburn. If the result is somewhat two-dimensional in personal terms, it is all the more powerful as an icon.

The concept of an Audrey Hepburn Type is so pervasive that casting agencies still use it today to specify the demands of a certain role. But when you look closely at the image of Audrey Hepburn over the years, you quickly see that it has changed repeatedly. The more you examine it, the harder it is to isolate the exact characteristics that make up the "Audrey Hepburn type."

When Hepburn burst on the screen in her first US movie, *Roman Holiday*, and promptly won an Oscar for it, her impact was enormous. Photos of her abounded; stills from the film; publicity photos in which she seemed somewhat ill at ease; long photo essays in *Life* and *Look* showing her at work on her second movie, *Sabrina*. The Hepburn of those first few years in the public eye – the time of *Gigi*, *Roman Holiday*, *Sabrina*, and *Ondine* – was definitely a gamine, an elf. It was her youth, her delicacy, her vulnerability that caught our imagination. She was called "coltish," "gazelle-like," "other-worldly" ("I guess they mean I'm tall and skinny," elucidated Hepburn wryly in an amusing interview). her eyes were "lake-haunted" ("Maybe I need sleep") under "bat-winged brows" ("I just don't pluck them"). Anita Loos pointed out that her waist, at 19½ inches, was smaller than her head (22 inches) adding, "During the Gay Nineties, the great Polaire was made famous by that single fact." (Polaire's choice of bedfellows may have had something to do with her fame too.) Edith Head said Hepburn had the slimmest waist since Scarlett O'Hara; it was so small "you could get a dog collar around it!" Much was made of her short uneven haircut. She herself said during the run of *Gigi*, "It seems to get messier and messier every year. I wear long hair in the play, you know, and it's something of a shock to me when I take it off and look in the mirror and see – this!"

THE HEPBURN IMAGE

Cecil Beaton, writing for *Vogue* in 1954, perceptively summed up her impact in those first few years. "No one can doubt that Audrey Hepburn's appearance succeeds because it embodies the spirit of today. She had, if you like, her prototypes in France – Dam Edith Piaf, or Juliette Greco. But it took the rubble of Belgium, an English accent, and an American success to launch the striking personality that best exemplifies our new *Zeitgeist*.

"Nobody ever looked like her before World War II; it is doubtful if anybody ever did, unless it be those wild children of the French Revolution who stride in the foreground of romantic canvases. Yet we recognize the rightness of this appearance in relation to our historical needs. And the proof is that thousands of imitations have appeared. The woods are full of emaciated young ladies with rat-nibbled hair and moon-pale faces.

"Audrey Hepburn is the *gamine*, the urchin, the lost Bernardo boy. Sometimes she appears to be dangerously fatigued; already, at her lettuce age, there are apt to be shadows under the eyes, while her cheeks seem taut and pallid. She is a wistful child of a war-chided era . . ."

But already there was a hint that this wistful child was to change into something else. Publicity photos that appeared between 1952 and 1954 showed us a girl who was almost deliberately removed from the sphere of fashion. She wore toreador pants and men's shirts, tied tight at the waist; the tights, bulky sweaters and small head scarves of the European student; coats distinguished by their obvious functionality. Interviewers at the time commented on the "refreshing simplicity" of her clothes rather than their chic. But in 1954, *Sabrina* was released. The movie was her first professional collaboration with French couturier Hubert de Givenchy, and in the scenes after Sabrina has been to Paris and turned herself into a sophisticate, we see the foreshadowing of the chic for which Hepburn was soon to become famous.

The movies that Hepburn made during the rest of the decade of the Fifties, after her marriage to Mel Ferrer, are the ones that typify her image of the child-woman. *Love in the Afternoon* and more particularly *Funny Face* (in both of which she was again dressed by Givenchy) played on this delicate balance between her look of a lost child — all eyes and jagged hair, like Dondi in the comic strips, or those tacky paintings by Walter Keane – and her European chic, her polished manners, her air of "good breeding," that seemed to come from an earlier age.

These movies continued her transformation from genuine gamine into a fashionable woman who had simply adopted a style based on the gamine look. *Funny Face* both exemplifies and exaggerates the transition by making her a bohemian, dressed all in high-minded a-fashionable black, in the early part of the movie, who blooms into a fashionplate midway through the plot.

Hepburn's face was an integral part of her elfin image in the Fifties. The eyebrows remained thick and dark, her skin surprisingly pale by contrast. Beaton described the way in which she intentionally achieved the face that lingers in our minds: "She wears no powder, so that her white skin has a bright sheen. Using a stick of grease paint with a deft stroke, she draws

heavy bars of black upon her naturally full brows, and almost in Fratellini fashion, liberally smudges both upper and lower eyelids with black. To complete the clown boldness, she enlarges her mouth even at the ends, thus making her smile expand to an enormous slice from Sambo's watermelon. The general public in its acceptance of such an uncompromisingly stark appearance has radically foresaken the prettily romantic or pseudo-mysterious heroines of only two decades ago."

As this quote suggests, one of the most interesting — and novel — aspects of the Hepburn image is the extent to which we understand that she has created her own appeal. Reporters loved to stress that "her teeth are not perfectly aligned, her nostrils flare, and her dark hair seems to be carelessly cut." Or, "Her nose is too little and her eyes are too big for anybody's beauty standards . . . her eyebrows, singly, are as thick as both lips together." One fan magazine article summed up the surprising appeal of this imperfect image: "If you are a woman, for instance, this is how you would like to be. Particularly if you are as imperfect as Audrey. By any beauty parlor or beauty contest standards, she is hopelessly ill-proportioned and unsymmetrical. Her teeth are crooked, her frame is lank, and yet somehow she comes off as a ravishingly beautiful girl. She is the living embodiment of that old adage about beauty being more than skin deep."

Hepburn's own remarks in interviews stressed this self-created aspects of her looks. She sometimes spoke of having felt ugly as a girl, and it was not just modesty that led her to downplay claims for her beauty. She candidly admitted that she had to work at looking attractive, and revealed the fact that there was a shrewd brain directing the choices that added up to the Hepburn look. She said, "You have to look at yourself objectively. Analyze yourself like an instrument. Ask yourself what it is suited for. You have to be absolutely frank with yourself, even when you consider a part. If I see a box of chocolates and I'm afraid I'd gain five pounds, I fight it. If I tear open the string on that box of candy, I'll eat it. So I don't open it, and fight my emotions. I guess it's a basic form of insecurity."

So another aspect of the Hepburn image was the ugly-duckling-swan transformation, and the audience frequently felt that they got to see it happen on the screen. Our participation makes the change that much more dramatic, as well as that much more convincing to us. The twist in this ugly-duckling story is that it's the duckling herself who is bringing about the change. Hepburn tells us frankly that she desciplined herself into that willowy figure, she invented the eye makeup that makes her face so striking, she deliberately struck those eye-catching poses, and she selected the ever more fashionable clothes that did so much for her image.

It is this aspect of intention, of careful intelligent planning and rigorous discipline, that makes Hepburn's image so modern. Previous movie queens liked to make themselves seem to be "naturally" attractive. You can't quite imagine Greta Garbo fussing over the exact arch of her eyebrow, or Doris Day spending hours on makeup to do the very best job of presenting her freckles attractively. Even Hepburn's contemporaries, other superstars such as Elizabeth Taylor and Sophia Loren, projected the sense that they were just

born that ravishing. But of course, common sense tells us that no one looks truly beautiful without a certain amount of effort and will — the right makeup, the most flattering hair style, the clothes that emphasize the body's best features — no matter what kind of assets one is born with. It is almost certain to be the case that Elizabeth Taylor has always spent just as much time and effort over her looks as Audrey Hepburn: the difference lies in the fact that Hepburn exaggerates it and Taylor minimizes it.

Hepburn's attitude doesn't seem particularly surprising today. We are used to the how-to books, the flood of magazine articles about making ourselves beautiful. But in the Fifties, there were still many remnants in the public consciousness of a much older, almost Puritanical, attitude. We were then only a scant generation away from a time when "painting your face" was scandalous at worst and bad taste at best. Only a "certain type of girl" desired to attract by her looks; respectable women lived by the motto "Pretty is as pretty does." Women of the Thirties and Forties wore makeup, they said, to "accentuate" their innate good looks, but Hepburn was modern enough to admit she used it to *create* them.

Throughout the decade of the Fifties, Hepburn's image retained a flavour of androgyny. That was partly the result of the short boyish haircut, partly the result of the lean flat-chested figure. It may also have been somewhat linked to the quality of will and determination she projected, both in her public and her private personae. Thirty years ago, we were not in the habit of regarding these as feminine qualities. The only other star who seemed capable of such a degree of determination was Joan Crawford, and she certainly managed (even *before* the publication of *Mommie Dearest*) to give willpower a bad name. There was always something repellent and obsessive about the nakedness of Crawford's desire to perfect herself. Hepburn's youth, her look of fragility, her air of good manners, softened the edges of her wilfullness; in her, it seemed plucky, gallant, a commendable effort on the part of one so vulnerable. In short, she feminized the previously masculine quality of great determination.

During the decade of the Sixties, Hepburn's image underwent another change. The elements of androgyny and childishness faded away; what was left was a grown woman of great elegance and style. The process started in *Breakfast at Tiffany's*. For the first time, the childish elements in the Hepburn character were seen as flaws. In earlier roles Hepburn had played, a childish streak made the heroines more attractive, but in Holly Golightly, at last the reverse was true.

In the films of the Fifties, the vulnerability of Hepburn characters came largely from within, from the heroine's child-like nature. In the Sixties, the vulnerabilities were imposed through the script. Hepburn played a woman who was blind, whose husband had just been murdered, who was involved in a crime through no fault of her own, who was suddenly transported into unfamiliar social circumstances, who was forced to rely on the help of a teacher or a mysterious protector. Through such plot devices, directors were able to continue using Hepburn's air of fragility and vulnerability even after she no longer exhibited any childlike aspects.

The maturity of Hepburn's characters was reflected by the maturity of her wardrobe, both on and off screen. This was the period when her relationship with Givenchy was at its zenith. She admitted, "I depend on Givenchy in the same way that American women depend on their psychiatrists." One element in this dependence emerged when she was told by Stanley Donen that he would not allow Givenchy to design her clothes for *Two for the Road*. She exclaimed in distress, "Why? Hubert makes me feel so sure of myself. I'll give a better performance in his clothes."

She had met the designer during her early modelling days in London, and first worked with him in *Sabrina*. Thereafter, he designed most of her movie wardrobes as well as her personal one, and in many ways the Audrey Hepburn look is really the Givenchy look. The two became close friends, and she said of him in 1965, "There are few people that I love more. He is the single person I know with the greatest integrity." Throughout the decade of the Sixties, their careers continued to be very much intertwined. He made her clothes for nearly all her films. He designed her son Sean's christening gown, as well as the dress Hepburn wore for the occasion. When she married Andrea Dotti, Givenchy made her wedding dress. Together, they set many styles – the shallow square neckline that is still called a Sabrina neckline, from a dress in that film; the sleeveless cocktail sheath, from *Breakfast at Tiffany's*; opaque black stockings (*Funny Face*) and patterned white stockings (*How To Steal A Million*). She made the prestigious best-dressed list three times in a row wearing his clothes in her personal life. And her devotion was, of course, good publicity for Givenchy, whose sales soared during the period. Many of the models he used to show his collection looked suspiciously like Audrey Hepburn. Their mutual admiration seems to have

reached its height in 1966, when he introduced to the public his perfume L'Interdit, by advertising the fact that it was created for her — with a huge portrait of her in the background of the ads.

Throughout most of the Sixties, Audrey Hepburn was probably second only to Jacqueline Kennedy in the amount of flattery in the form of imitation she received. Popular magazines carried layouts that explained how to set your hair to look like Audrey Hepburn, how to do the exercises that Audrey Hepburn invented to stay in shape, how to use Audrey Hepburn's tips for buying clothes and building a wardrobe. Glossier periodicals like *Vogue* carried long feature stories on her taste in clothes, the way she lived at home. Daily papers featured photos of her in the latest Givenchy styles. She became identified in the public mind as a sort of classy clothes horse, an impression enhanced by the interviews she gave. She told the *New York Times*, "I always dreamt of the day when I would have enough closets — big ones. Some people dream of having a big swimming pool — with me, it's closets."

This image of Hepburn was at its most pervasive around the time she remarried and retired for a period into the concerns of home and family. When she re-emerged in the mid-Seventies, she seemed to have changed again. Today, her figure is as spare and angular as ever, but her face is softer, considerably closer to the traditional definition of feminine prettiness than it used to be. Much of the change comes from the way she now makes up her eyes. At the time of the filming of *My Fair Lady*, Cecil Beaton stressed the effect of the eye makeup she then employed. One day, he said, "a singing voice invited me to 'Come on in and see my secrets.' It was Audrey in the Makeup Department. 'Now, you see, I have no eyes.' Without the usual mascara and shadow, however, Audrey's eyes are like those in a Flemish painting and are even more appealing — young and sad. Yet it was extraordinary to see that it is simply by painting her eyes she has become a beauty in the modern sense." She no longer uses the heavy black eyeliner, and even the eyeshadow and mascara are lighter. Moreover, her eyebrows, once so thick and black, have been thinned, by time or artifice. The change in her eyes, coupled with a new softly curly hair style, creates an image of gentle femininity.

Her wardrobe on the screen emphasizes this new aspect of her image. Although her clothes are still stylish (and still largely by Givenchy) they are no longer so extreme, so stark. Her necklines now have gently draped cowl collars, she wears a fluffy muffler with her man-tailored jacket. Even the materials seem softer; instead of hard-finish gabardine and twill, there are fuzzy sweaters, velvet pants. And the colors are warmer. She is no longer so likely to be wearing high-contrast black and white, but muted beiges, heathery blues, colors that blend together almost imperceptibly.

It is almost certainly the case that the successive changes in the Hepburn image were the result of necessity as much as choice. After all, she couldn't be a child eternally. As she grew up, she had to drop the childish element that was a part of her initial image; as she grew older, she had to drop the hard-outline, high-contrast chic that tends to make older women look unpleasantly frozen and haggard. But whatever the cause, the result has been a clear progression toward the feminine pole. In her youth, she was boyish, sometimes asexual, often at least pre-sexual. Later she became more obviously sexual in her image, but at the same time somewhat remote and unapproachable in her haute couture elegance. Only recently has the image of Audrey Hepburn become fully womanly.

There is a corollary to this development; along with the visual change has come an emotional one. The early Audrey Hepburn seemed *physically* vulnerable. She had a child's air of being only just in control of the suddenly long limbs, big feet, and increasing height of approaching adulthood. She might sometimes be sad, but we always expected that, like a child, she would be quickly cheered up when something good came along. The only emotional risks she ran were those of naivete. But for the current Hepburn persona, the vulnerability is all *emotional*; it is, in fact, the vulnerability of traditional womanhood. You feel instinctively that these heroines can truly be hurt by affairs of the heart, by the faithlessness of a lover, by the phone that doesn't ring, by the trust that isn't repaid. Moreover, you also intuit that when these hurts are inflicted, full recovery is no longer possible.

So in the final analysis, perhaps the most amazing thing about the Audrey Hepburn Type is that it is *not* a static image, but one that is fully capable of growing and changing. Unlike n..ny successful stars, Hepburn has not formed a hard outer shell of the style that took her to the height of success and then quietly decayed from within. Rather, she has changed the style in response to both her own physical changes and — perhaps more important — changes in the way society looks at the feminine role.

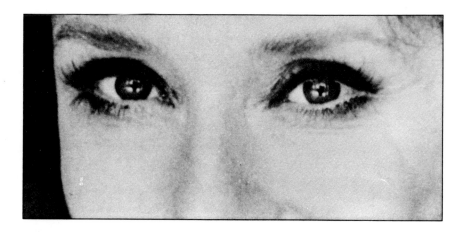

FILMOGRAPHY

One Wild Oat
Eros-Coronet 1951
DIRECTOR: Charles Saunders
PRODUCER:
SCREENPLAY: Vernon Sylvaine and Lawrence Huntington from Sylvaine's play
RUNNING TIME: 78 minutes
CAST: Robertson Hare, Stanley Holloway, Constance Lorne, Vera Pearce, June
Sylvaine, Audrey Hepburn in a bit part

Young Wives' Tale
Associated British/Allied Artists 1951
DIRECTOR: Henry Cass
PRODUCER:
SCREENPLAY: Anne Burnaby from the play by Ronald Jeans
RUNNING TIME: 78 minutes
CAST: Joan Greenwood, Nigel Patrick, Derek Farr, Bruce Middleton, Athene Seyler,
Helen Cherry, Audrey Hepburn in a small part

Laughter in Paradise
Associated British/Pathé 1951
DIRECTOR: Mario Zampi
PRODUCER:
SCREENPLAY: Michael Pertwee and Jack Davies
RUNNING TIME: 97 minutes
CAST: Alastair Sim, Fay Compton, Guy Middleton, George Cole, Hugh Griffith, Ernest
Thesiger, Beatrice Campbell, Mackenzie Ward, A.E. Mathews, Joyce Grenfell, Audrey
Hepburn in a bit part

The Lavender Hill Mob
Rank/Universal 1951
DIRECTOR: Charles Crichton
PRODUCER:
SCREENPLAY: T.E.B. Clarke
RUNNING TIME: 81 minutes
CAST: Alec Guinness, Stanley Holloway, Sidney James, Alfie Bass, Marjorie Fielding,
Edie Martin, John Salew, Audrey Hepburn in a bit part

The Secret People
Ealing/Lippert 1952
DIRECTOR: Thorold Dickinson
PRODUCER:
SCREENPLAY: Thorold Dickinson and Wolfgang Wilhelm from an original story by
Dickinson and Joyce Cary
RUNNING TIME: 86 minutes
CAST: Valentina Cortesa, Serge Reggiani, Charles Goldner, Megs Jenkins, Irene
Worth, Audrey Hepburn

Monte Carlo Baby
Ventura/Filmakers 1953
DIRECTORS: Jean Boyer and Jean Jerrold
PRODUCER: Ray Ventura
SCREENPLAY: Jean Jarrold, Alex Jaffe and Jean Boyer
RUNNING TIME: 70 minutes
CAST: Jules Munshin, Michelle Farmer, Cara Williams, Philippe LeMaire, Russell
Collins, John Van Dreelan, Audrey Hepburn, Ray Ventura and his orchestra

Roman Holiday
Paramount 1953
DIRECTOR: William Wyler
PRODUCER:
SCREENPLAY: Ian McLellan Hunter and John Dighton from an original play by Hunter
RUNNING TIME: 118 minutes
CAST: Gregory Peck, Audrey Hepburn, Eddie Albert, Hartley Power, Harcourt
Williams, Margaret Rawlings

Sabrina
Paramount 1954
DIRECTOR: Billy Wilder
PRODUCER: Billy Wilder
SCREENPLAY: Billy Wilder, Samuel Taylor and Ernest Lehman from Taylor's play
Sabrina Fair
RUNNING TIME: 112 minutes
CAST: Humphrey Bogart, Audrey Hepburn, William Holden, Walter Hampden, John
Williams, Martha Hyer, Joan Vohs, Francis X. Bushman, Ellen Corby, Nancy Kulp

War and Peace
Ponti-DeLaurentiis/Paramount 1956
DIRECTOR: King Vidor
PRODUCER: Dino DeLaurentiis
SCREENPLAY: Brigit Boland, Robert Westerby, King Vidor, Mario Camerini, Ennio
DeConcini and Ivo Perilli from the novel by Leo Tolstoy
RUNNING TIME: 208 minutes
CAST: Audrey Hepburn, Henry Fonda, Mel Ferrer, Vittorio Gassman, Herbert Lom,
Oscar Homolka, Anita Ekberg, Helmut Dantine, Barry Jones, Jeremy Brett, May
Britt, John Mills

Funny Face
Paramount 1957
DIRECTOR: Stanley Donen
PRODUCER: Roger Edens
SCREENPLAY: Leonard Gershe
MUSIC AND LYRICS: George and Ira Gershwin from the 1927 Broadway musical of the
same name, additional music and lyrics by Leonard Gershe and Roger Edens
RUNNING TIME: 103 minutes
CAST: Audrey Hepburn, Fred Astaire, Kay Thompson, Michael Arclair, Robert
Flemyng, Dovima, Suzy Parker, Virginia Gibson, Sunny Harnett, Ruta Lee

Love in the Afternoon
Allied Artists 1957
DIRECTOR: Billy Wilder
PRODUCER: Billy Wilder
SCREENPLAY: Billy Wilder and I.A.L. Diamond, based on the novel *Ariane* by
Claude Anet
RUNNING TIME: 125 minutes
CAST: Gary Cooper, Audrey Hepburn, Maurice Chevalier, John McGiver, Van Doude,
Lise Bourdin

Green Mansions
Metro-Goldwyn-Mayer 1959
DIRECTOR: Mel Ferrer
PRODUCER: Edmund Grainger
SCREENPLAY: Dorothy Kingsley, based on the novel by W.H. Hudson
RUNNING TIME: 104 minutes
CAST: Audrey Hepburn, Anthony Perkins, Lee J. Cobb, Sessue Hayakawa, Henry Silva,
Nehemiah Persoff

The Nun's Story
Warner Brothers 1959
DIRECTOR: Fred Zinneman
PRODUCER: Henry Blake
SCREENPLAY: Robert Anderson, from the book by Kathryn C. Hulme
RUNNING TIME: 149 minutes
CAST: Audrey Hepburn, Peter Finch, Dame Edith Evans, Dame Peggy Ashcroft, Dean
Jagger, Mildred Dunnock, Beatrice Straight, Rosalie Crutchley, Colleen Dewhurst

The Unforgiven
Hecht-Hill-Lancaster/United Artists 1960
DIRECTOR: John Huston
PRODUCER: Burt Lancaster
SCREENPLAY: Ben Maddow, based on the novel by Alan LeMay
RUNNING TIME: 125 minutes
CAST: Burt Lancaster, Audrey Hepburn, Audie Murphy, John Saxon, Charles
Bickford, Lillian Gish, Albert Salmi, Joseph Wiseman, June Walker, Doug McClure

Breakfast at Tiffany's
Jurow-Shepherd/Paramount 1961
DIRECTOR: Blake Edwards
PRODUCERS: Martin Jurow and Richard Shepherd
SCREENPLAY: George Axelrod, based on the novella by Truman Capote
RUNNING TIME: 115 minutes
CAST: Audrey Hepburn, George Peppard, Patricia Neal, Mickey Rooney, Buddy Ebsen,
Martin Balsam, Jose-Luis de Villalonga, John McGiver, Alan Reed, Dorothy Whitney

The Children's Hour
Mirisch/United Artists
DIRECTOR: William Wyler
PRODUCER: William Wyler
SCREENPLAY: John Michael Hayes from Lillian Hellman's adaptation of her own play
RUNNING TIME: 109 minutes
CAST: Audrey Hepburn, Shirley MacLaine, James Garner, Miriam Hopkins, Fay
Bainter, Karen Balkin, Veronica Cartwright, Mimi Gibson

Charade
Universal 1963
DIRECTOR: Stanley Donen
PRODUCER: Stanley Donen
SCREENPLAY: Peter Stone, from the story "The Unsuspecting Wife" by Stone and
Marc Behm
RUNNING TIME: 113 minutes
CAST: Audrey Hepburn, Cary Grant, Walter Matthau, James Coburn, George Kennedy,
Ned Glass, Jacques Marin, Paul Bonifas

Paris When It Sizzles
Paramount 1961
DIRECTOR: Richard Quine
PRODUCER: Richard Quine and George Axelrod
SCREENPLAY: George Axelrod, from a story and screenplay by Julien Duvivier and
Henri Jeanson
RUNNING TIME: 110 minutes
CAST: Audrey Hepburn, William Holden, Gregoire Aslan, Noel Coward, the voices of
Fred Astaire and Frank Sinatra. Cameo appearances by Marlene Dietrich, Tony
Curtis, and Mel Ferrer

My Fair Lady
Warner Brothers 1964
DIRECTOR: George Cukor
PRODUCER: Jack Warner
SCREENPLAY: Alan Jay Lerner, from his stage adaptation of George Bernard Shaw's
play *Pygmalion*
RUNNING TIME: 170 minutes
CAST: Audrey Hepburn, Rex Harrison, Stanley Holloway, Wilfrid Hyde-White, Gladys
Cooper, Jeremy Brett, Theodore Bikel, Mona Washbourne, Isobel Elsom, John
Holland, Henry Daniell, Grady Sutton

How To Steal A Million
Twentieth-Century-Fox 1966
DIRECTOR: William Wyler
PRODUCER: William Wyler
SCREENPLAY: Harry Kurnitz, from a story by George Bradshaw
RUNNING TIME: 127 minutes
CAST: Audrey Hepburn, Peter O'Toole, Eli Wallach, Hugh Griffith, Charles Boyer,
Fernard Gravey, Marcel Dalio

Two for the Road
Twentieth-Century-Fox 1967
DIRECTOR: Stanley Donen
PRODUCER: Stanley Donen
SCREENPLAY: Frederic Raphael
RUNNING TIME: 112 minutes
CAST: Audrey Hepburn, Albert Finney, Eleanor Bron, William Daniels, Claude
Dauphin, Nadia Grey, Jacqueline Bisset in a bit part

Wait Until Dark
Warner Brothers 1967
DIRECTOR: Terence Young
PRODUCER: Mel Ferrer
SCREENPLAY: Robert and Jane Howard Carrington, based on Frederick Knott's play
RUNNING TIME: 108 minutes
CAST: Audrey Hepburn, Alan Arkin, Richard Crenna, Efrem Zimbalist, Jr., Jack
Weston, Samantha Jones, Julie Herrod

Robin and Marian
Columbia Pictures 1976
DIRECTOR: Richard Lester
PRODUCER: Ray Stark
SCREENPLAY: James Goldman
RUNNING TIME: 106 minutes
CAST: Audrey Hepburn, Sean Connery, Robert Shaw, Nicol Williamson, Richard
Harris, Kenneth Haigh, Ian Holm, Denholm Elliott

Bloodline
Paramount 1979
DIRECTOR: Terence Young
PRODUCERS: David V. Picker and Sidney Beckerman
SCREENPLAY: Laird Koenig, from the novel by Sidney Sheldon
RUNNING TIME: 116 minutes
CAST: Audrey Hepburn, Ben Gazzara, James Mason, Claudia Mori, Irene Papas,
Michelle Phillips, Maurice Ronet, Romy Schneider, Omar Sharif, Beatrice Straight,
Gert Frobe

They All Laughed
Moon Pictures 1981
DIRECTOR: Peter Bogdanovich
PRODUCERS: George Morfogen and Blaine Novak
SCREENPLAY: Peter Bogdanovich
RUNNING TIME: 113 minutes
CAST: Audrey Hepburn, Ben Gazzara, John Ritter, Colleen Camp, Dorothy Stratton,
Patti Hanson, George Morfogen, Blaine Novak, Sean Ferrer, and Antonia and
Alexandra Bogdanovich